Cambridge Elements

Elements in Ethics
edited by
Ben Eggleston
University of Kansas
Dale E. Miller
Old Dominion University, Virginia

MORAL RESPONSIBILITY RECONSIDERED

Gregg D. Caruso
SUNY Corning

Derk Pereboom
Cornell University

CAMBRIDGE
UNIVERSITY PRESS

Shaftesbury Road, Cambridge CB2 8EA, United Kingdom

One Liberty Plaza, 20th Floor, New York, NY 10006, USA

477 Williamstown Road, Port Melbourne, VIC 3207, Australia

314–321, 3rd Floor, Plot 3, Splendor Forum, Jasola District Centre,
New Delhi – 110025, India

103 Penang Road, #05–06/07, Visioncrest Commercial, Singapore 238467

Cambridge University Press is part of Cambridge University Press & Assessment,
a department of the University of Cambridge.

We share the University's mission to contribute to society through the pursuit of
education, learning and research at the highest international levels of excellence.

www.cambridge.org
Information on this title: www.cambridge.org/9781009219754

DOI: 10.1017/9781009219730

First published 2022

A catalogue record for this publication is available from the British Library.

ISBN 978-1-009-21975-4 Paperback
ISSN 2516-4031 (online)
ISSN 2516-4023 (print)

Moral Responsibility Reconsidered

Elements in Ethics

DOI: 10.1017/9781009219730
First published online: November 2022

Gregg D. Caruso
SUNY Corning

Derk Pereboom
Cornell University

Author for correspondence: Gregg D. Caruso, gcaruso@corning-cc.edu

Abstract: This Element examines the concept of moral responsibility as it is used in contemporary philosophical debates and explores the justifiability of the moral practices associated with it, including moral praise/blame, retributive punishment, and the reactive attitudes of resentment and indignation. After identifying and discussing several different varieties of responsibility – including *causal responsibility*, *take-charge responsibility*, *role responsibility*, *liability responsibility*, and the kinds of responsibility associated with *attributability*, *answerability*, and *accountability* – it distinguishes between *basic* and *non-basic desert* conceptions of moral responsibility and considers a number of skeptical arguments against each. It then outlines an alternative forward-looking account of moral responsibility grounded in non-desert-invoking desiderata such as protection, reconciliation, and moral formation. It concludes by addressing concerns about the practical implications of skepticism about desert-based moral responsibility and explains how *optimistic skeptics* can preserve most of what we care about when it comes to our interpersonal relationships, morality, and meaning in life.

Keywords: moral responsibility, free will, free will skepticism, basic desert, forward-looking moral responsibility

ISBNs: 9781009219754 (PB), 9781009219730 (OC)
ISSNs: 2516-4031 (online), 2516-4023 (print)

Contents

1 Moral Responsibility

A fundamental and familiar part of our personal relationships and our everyday moral practices is making judgments about whether a person is morally responsible for their behavior, and, when we judge that they are, holding them responsible for their actions and omissions. We typically think, for instance, that non-human animals, very young children, and those suffering from severe developmental disabilities or dementia do not satisfy the conditions for moral responsibility. On the other hand, when a normal adult human being knowingly does wrong, it is natural to think that they are (absent any excusing conditions) morally responsible for what they did and therefore deserving of certain negative attitudes, judgments, and treatment. Similarly, when someone does something morally right or exemplary, and we judge they are competent, uncoerced, and aware of what they are doing, we feel that they are deserving of praise and reward. Philosophers, however, have long debated whether individuals are ever morally responsible in this sense and whether our common practice of holding individuals responsible and legitimate targets of various desert-based attitudes, judgments, and treatment is ever justified.

This Element introduces and examines the concept of moral responsibility as it is used in contemporary philosophical debates, and explores the justifiability of the moral practices associated with it, including moral praise and blame, retributive punishment, and the reactive attitudes of resentment, indignation, and, more broadly, moral anger. It begins by identifying and discussing several different varieties of responsibility, including *causal responsibility, take-charge responsibility, role responsibility, liability responsibility*, and the kinds of responsibility associated with *attributability, answerability*, and *accountability*. It then argues that the kind of moral responsibility that is of central philosophical and practical importance in the free will and moral responsibility debates is best understood in terms of *basic desert*, the idea that the harm of blame and punishment and the benefit of praise and reward are deserved and fundamentally so, and that such backward-looking desert is thus a basic element of morality. We (your authors) deny that human beings are ever morally responsible in this basic desert sense, and we accordingly advocate *skepticism* about basic desert. However, we also contend that forward-looking aspects of our practice of holding morally responsible, those that feature aims such as reconciliation in relationships and moral formation of wrongdoers, are justified. Thus, upon reconsidering moral responsibility, we argue that certain backward-looking aspects should be rejected, and certain forward-looking aspects retained.

In this Element we will examine the arguments for basic desert skepticism. Some skeptics deny that we have basic desert moral responsibility because they believe it can be shown to be incoherent or impossible. Others maintain that although this sort of responsibility is coherent and possible, nevertheless, our best philosophical and scientific theories provide compelling reasons for denying that we have it. Often basic desert skeptics contend that we lack the control in action, that is, the *free will*, basic desert moral responsibility requires. Accordingly, they are also typically skeptics about an important and controversial sort of free will.[1] What all basic desert skeptics agree on, however, is that adequate justification for grounding basic desert moral responsibility and the practices associated with it – basic desert-invoking praise and blame, punishment and reward – has not been produced (Pereboom 2001, 2014a, 2021b; Levy 2011; Waller 2011, 2014; Caruso 2012, 2018b, 2021b).

Critics tend to focus both on the arguments for skepticism about basic desert and on its practical implications. Some reject the claim that basic desert moral responsibility is incompatible with determinism, and are also concerned that accepting the skeptical position would mistakenly result in people not getting what they deserve. Some argue that rejecting basic desert moral responsibility would have damaging consequences for morality, the law, society, personal relationships, and our sense of meaning in life. They contend, for instance, that it would undermine morality, leave us unable to adequately deal with criminal behavior, increase anti-social conduct, and jeopardize our sense of achievement and purpose. *Optimistic skeptics* respond by arguing that rejecting basic desert moral responsibility would not be destructive in these ways. They argue that threats to morality can be averted, and that prospects for sustaining good personal relationships and our sense of meaning in life can be vindicated. Although retributivism as a justification for criminal punishment would be ruled out, adequate resources for dealing with criminal behavior remain in place.

1.1 Varieties of Responsibility

When philosophers discuss moral responsibility, what they generally have in mind is the kind of responsibility that makes agents justified targets of certain approving or disapproving attitudes, judgment, and treatment. As we've noted,

---

[1] Historical advocates of skepticism about this sort of free will include Śāntideva (700/1995), Spinoza (1677/1985), Paul d'Holbach (1770), Joseph Priestley (1778/1965), Arthur Schopenhauer (1818/1961), Friedrich Nietzsche (1888/1954). More recent proponents include Galen Strawson (1986, 1994), Ted Honderich (1988), Bruce Waller (1990, 2011, 2015), Michael Slote (1990), Derk Pereboom (1995, 2001, 2014a, 2021b), Saul Smilansky (2000), Daniel Wegner (2002), Gideon Rosen (2004), Joshua Greene and Jonathan Cohen (2004), Benjamin Vilhauer (2004, 2012), Shaun Nichols (2007, 2015), Tamler Sommers (2007, 2012), Brian Leiter (2007), Thomas Nadelhoffer (2011), Neil Levy (2011), Sam Harris (2012), Gregg Caruso (2012, 2021b), 'Trick Slattery (2014), Per-Erik Milam (2016), Robert Sapolsky (2017), Stephen Morris (2018), Elizabeth Shaw (2019), and Farah Focquaert (2019b); for an overview, see Caruso (2018b).

our practice of holding agents morally responsible has backward- and forward-looking aspects. The core backward-looking aspect is desert – in particular, the deserved harm of blame and punishment for wrongdoing, and the deserved benefit of praise and reward for morally exemplary action. A basic conception of desert is backward-looking to its core. That is, basic desert claims are fundamental, and thus not grounded on forward-looking considerations such as reconciliation in relationships and moral formation of wrongdoers.

One concern raised for skepticism about basic desert is that it is too revisionary of our moral responsibility practices. A more conciliatory and conservative position, defended by Daniel Dennett and Manuel Vargas, aims to ground our moral responsibility practice, inclusive of its desert-based justifications, in forward-looking considerations at a higher level. On such accounts, practice-level justifications for blame and punishment invoke considerations of desert, while that desert is not basic because at a higher level the practice is justified by good anticipated consequences, such as deterrence of wrongdoing and moral formation of wrongdoers. Defenders of this approach maintain that our practice of holding agents morally responsible in this non-basic desert sense should be retained for the reason that doing so would have the best overall consequences relative to alternative practices. While such a view avoids certain objections to basic desert, it faces a number of other concerns (see Section 1.3). As an alternative, we will set out in Section 3 our more resolutely forward-looking conception of moral responsibility, grounded in objectives such as moral formation of wrongdoers and reconciliation in relationships impaired by wrongdoing (Pereboom 1995, 2001, 2014a, 2021b; Caruso 2021b; Caruso in Dennett and Caruso 2021).

To begin, it is important that we first differentiate *moral* responsibility, whether backward- or forward-looking, from several other notions of responsibility. In fact, the term "responsibility" is perhaps surprisingly ambiguous and used in a number of different senses. Sometimes, for instance, we use it to simply indicate the cause of something – as when we say that "Hurricane Katrina was responsible for the destruction of New Orleans" or "The fallen tree branch was responsible for the damage to the roof." This sense, known as *causal responsibility*, is assigned when we say that someone or something is responsible for an event or outcome because he, she, or it caused it to occur (Talbert 2016: 8). Inanimate objects (such as the tree branch) and events (like Hurricane Katrina) can be causally responsible in this sense. So too can agents when they play a direct or indirect causal role in bringing about a particular action or outcome. Note, though, that causal responsibility is far from sufficient for moral responsibility – someone or something can cause an event or outcome without deserving moral praise or blame, punishment or reward, for having done so. This is easiest to see in the case of inanimate objects and events, but it's also true for agents. An infant, for instance, may be causally responsible for ruining your favorite shirt by getting sick on it, and a Parkinson's patient for knocking your cell phone to the ground because of their tremors, even though neither is morally responsible for what they did.

Moral responsibility is also distinct from *take-charge responsibility* (Waller 1990, 2004, 2011, 2014). Skeptic Bruce Waller argues that:

> Just deserts and moral responsibility require a godlike power – the existential power of choosing ourselves, the godlike power of making ourselves from scratch, the divine capacity to be an uncaused cause – that we do not have. (2011: 40)

Yet, Waller maintains,

> you [nevertheless] have take-charge responsibility for your own life, which is a responsibility you deeply value and enjoy exercising. (2011: 108)

Taking responsibility is distinguished from *being morally responsible* in that, if one takes responsibility for a particular outcome it does not follow that one is morally responsible for that outcome. One can take responsibility for many things, from the mundane to the vitally important. For example, one can take responsibility for teaching a course, organizing a conference, or throwing a birthday party. The responsibility taken, however, is very different from the moral responsibility that would justify blame and punishment, praise and reward (Pereboom 2001: xxi; Waller 2011: 105; for an objection, see Smilansky 2012; for a reply, see Caruso 2018b: sect. 1).

A closely related notion is what H.L.A. Hart designates as *role responsibility*. In introducing the idea, Hart points out that:

> Whenever a person occupies a distinctive place or office in a social organization, to which specific duties are attached to provide for the welfare of others or to advance in some specific way the aims or purposes of the organization, he is properly said to be responsible for the performance of these duties, or for doing what is necessary to fulfill them. Such duties are a person's [role] responsibility. (1968: 212)

We can say, then, that role responsibility refers to the various tasks and duties associated with a particular role or job description, such as being a parent, teacher, or firefighter. Such responsibility, however, does not entail moral responsibility. Autonomous machines and AI, for instance, can be responsible in the role sense since they are typically responsible for carrying out various tasks and duties in virtue of the roles for which they are designed. Just as we say that the surgeon, firefighter, or bridge inspector has certain "responsibilities" in virtue of their role or job description, we can say that an autonomous lunar rover or an AI used to locate and detonate landmines is "responsible" for performing specific tasks and achieving specific aims and purposes. Role responsibility, then, unlike moral responsibility, is to be understood in terms of the various tasks and actions necessary to fulfill a particular role or job description.

Civil liability is also distinct from moral responsibility. Civil liability is a legal obligation that requires a party to pay for damages or to follow other court-enforcements in a lawsuit. In a car crash case, for instance, the injured party can sue the driver and ask for monetary damages. A civil liability is usually a contractual liability or a tort liability. A tort, for instance, is something that occurs when one person's negligence directly causes property or personal damage to another – and it need not be intentional. An example of an unintentional tort would be someone being injured by a faulty product or someone's pet. As general rule, in tort law the financial harm suffered by the victim as a result of a tort is the only issue. Tort law attempts to adjust for harms done by awarding damages to a successful plaintiff who demonstrates that the defendant was the cause of the plaintiff's losses. Criminal law, on the other hand, is concerned with more than such restitution and compensation. It is also concerned with punishing wrongdoers for their criminal acts, not just as an act of restitution but as an expression of the state's disapproval of both the offense and the offender. Skeptics who reject basic desert moral responsibility can retain civil liability because the restitution and compensation of victims can be justified by appealing to the rights of those harmed together with weaker notions of responsibility, including causal responsibility. That is, civil liability need not assume agents are blameworthy and morally responsible in the basic desert sense, only that they are in a weaker sense responsible for some negligent act that caused harm and are therefore responsible, in the civil liability sense, for compensating victims.

In recent decades, philosophers have also drawn distinctions within the concept of moral responsibility. Prominently, some distinguish *attributability*, *answerability*, and *accountability* senses of moral responsibility. The first of these, attributability-responsibility, concerns actions or attitudes being properly attributable to, or reflective of, an agent's self. That is, we are responsible for our actions in the attributability sense when those actions reflect our nature or identity as moral agents, i.e., when they in this sense are attributable to us (Watson 1996; Eshleman 2014). Attributability-responsibility, however, makes no appeal to desert or backward-looking praise and blame, and hence it is distinct from any desert-invoking sense of moral responsibility. A particular action or attitude may be attributable to me in that it reflects on me, on my deep self, and in particular on who I am as an agent in the world, even if I am not deserving of praise and blame, punishment and reward for it. David Shoemaker

(2011, 2015) discusses numerous cases in which agents fail to be morally responsible in the desert-based sense – due to, for example, mental illness, clinical depression, or psychopathy – even though it remains appropriate to attribute various actions, attitudes, and characteristics to them.

Since attributability-responsibility does not depend on desert, it is also consistent with skepticism about basic desert moral responsibility. Consider the views on these issues of the great physicist Albert Einstein. In a 1929 interview in *The Saturday Evening Post*, he said: "I do not believe in free will . . . I believe with Schopenhauer: we can do what we wish, but we can only wish what we must." He then went on to add: "My own career was undoubtedly determined, not by my own will but by various factors over which I have no control." He concludes the interview by rejecting the idea that he deserved praise or credit for his scientific achievements: "I claim credit for nothing. Everything is determined, the beginning as well as the end, by forces over which we have no control." While free will and basic desert skeptics may agree with Einstein that he does not deserve praise for his various attributes and accomplishments, they can nevertheless attribute various attributes and accomplishments to him without inconsistency. We can say, for instance, that Einstein was an *exceptionally original thinker* and *extraordinarily intellectually creative* without presupposing that he was basically deserving of praise for any of those attributes (Caruso 2017).

The *answerability* sense of responsibility, defended by T.M. Scanlon (1998), Hilary Bok (1998), and Angela Smith (2012), is also claimed by some skeptics to be consistent with the rejection of basic desert moral responsibility (e.g., Pereboom 2014a, 2021b; Pereboom and Caruso 2018; Caruso 2021b; cf. Jeppsson 2016). In this sense of responsibility, someone is responsible for an action or attitude just in case it is connected to their capacity for evaluative judgment in a way that opens them up, in principle, to demands for justification from others. If an agent is answerability-responsible for a wrongdoing, it means we can legitimately ask him, "Why did you decide to do that?" or "Do you think it was the right thing to do?" Such questions target the deliberative, reasons-tracking aspects of agents. That is, "To be answerable . . . is to be susceptible for assessment of, and response to, the reasons one takes to justify one's actions" (Shoemaker 2011: 623). The sorts of answers the agent gives stand to reveal their reasons for action, what they take to be important, and salient aspects of their moral character, and subsequent responses may take the form of a demand for apology or a request for reform with the aim of modifying the wrongdoer's moral attitudes and dispositions (Shoemaker 2011: 623; Pereboom 2014a, 2021b).

We will have much more to say about this notion of responsibility (see Section 3), but for now we'll add two points about answerability-responsibility. First, it is distinct from, and not coextensive with, attributability-responsibility, since there are cases where an attitude or action is attributable to an agent without that agent being answerable for it (Shoemaker 2011, 2015). This can occur in cases when emotional commitments operate independently of evaluative reasons. In such circumstances, agents' attitudes or actions reflect on them, on their deep selves, and on who they are as agents in the world, but they would not be answerable for them. Second, an agent's answerability for an action does not entail moral responsibility for it in the basic desert sense. As we'll see in Section 3, there are ways to ground answerability and its demands for justification in forward-looking considerations independent of desert of any type. Answerability-responsibility should thus be understood to be distinct from basic desert moral responsibility.

The final sense of moral responsibility in this tripartite distinction is *accountability*. Accountability-responsibility is the responsibility that philosophers typically have in mind when they debate desert-based moral responsibility, the kind that makes an agent an appropriate target of various desert-based sanctions and rewards, including the reactive attitudes of resentment and indignation, and retributive punishment.

Shoemaker specifies that to hold someone to account for wrongdoing is "precisely to sanction that person, whether it be via the expression of a reactive attitude, public shaming, or something more psychologically or physically damaging" (Shoemaker 2011: 623). Whereas the answerability sense of moral responsibility is open to free will and basic desert skeptics to endorse, the accountability sense, at least as standardly characterized, is not, since it is typically set out as licensing responses such as resentment, indignation, and retribution (Watson 1996; Shoemaker 2011, 2015). We maintain that it is the accountability sense of moral responsibility, specifically when it is conceived as involving such responses as basically deserved, that separates the parties in the debate.

1.2 Desert-Based Moral Responsibility

Moral responsibility applies primarily to actions and omissions. We understand "action" to denote not only intentional bodily movements, but also to purely mental items such as decisions. To say that one is morally responsible for a good or bad action or omission, in the desert-based sense, is to say that one *deserves* to be praised or blamed, rewarded or punished, for that action. This may include the expression of certain attitudes and judgments, like resentment and indignation, or extend upward to more severe forms of retributive punishment. As Randolph Clarke explains:

> If any agent is truly [morally] responsible ... that fact provides us with a specific type of justification for responding in various ways to that agent,

with reactive attitudes of certain sorts, with praise or blame, with finite rewards or punishments. To be a morally responsible human agent is to be truly deserving of these sorts of responses, and deserving in a way that no agent is who is not responsible. This type of desert has a specific scope and force – one that distinguishes the justification for holding someone responsible from, say, the fairness of a grade given for a performance or any justification provided by consequences. (2005: 21)

This way of conceiving of our practice of holding people morally responsible goes back to P. F. Strawson's (1962) famous account of the *reactive attitudes*. According to Strawson, in the face of interpersonal wrongdoing it is both natural and justified to express certain types of anger; specially, *resentment*, directed toward someone due to a wrong done to oneself, and *indignation*, the vicarious analogue of resentment, directed toward someone because of a wrong done to a third party (Watson 1987; Wallace 1994; McKenna 2012; Shabo 2012; Brink 2021). Resentment and indignation, in Strawson's terminology, qualify as reactive attitudes.

These reactive attitudes are often accompanied by the supposition that its target *deserves* to be the recipient of the expression of such emotions. For instance, in the face of wrongdoing, one might express a kind of anger or blame, one that intentionally causes pain or harm, because it is believed that the wrongdoer deserves such pain or harm. A paradigm example would be when we confront a wrongdoer with expressions of angry blame (Wolf 2011; Fricker 2016; Bagley 2017; Shoemaker 2018; McKenna 2019). Such blame is associated with a certain negative emotional attitude toward the wrongdoer – such as resentment or indignation; and more broadly, moral anger – that goes beyond the mere absence or withdrawal of good will (Wolf 2011: 335). This kind of moral blame is non-trivially painful or harmful, and, when accompanied with a supposition of desert, qualifies as retributive. The positive counterpart of such blame is deserved praise and reward for good behavior.

When philosophers debate moral responsibility, it is typically this kind of desert-based moral responsibility they have in mind. Note, though, that the kind of "desert" operative here could be understood in either a *basic* or *non-basic* sense. In the basic form of desert, an agent deserves the harm or pain of blame or punishment just because he acted wrongly, given that he was aware or should have been aware that the action was wrong. An agent deserves the benefit or pleasure of praise or reward just because she acted in a morally exemplary way, given awareness of the moral status of the act (the account can be extended to omissions). The desert invoked here is basic because these claims about what agents deserve are fundamental in the sense that they are not justified by further considerations such as the good consequences of implementing them, or the provisions of an agreed-upon social contract (Feinberg 1970; Strawson 1994; Clarke 2005; Fischer 2007; Levy 2011; Scanlon 2013; Caruso and Morris 2017; Caruso 2021b; Dennett and Caruso 2021; Pereboom 2021b: 11–12, cf. 2001, 2014a: 2). The imposition of basically deserved pain or harm, pleasure or benefit, is in addition conceived as non-instrumentally good since such imposition is not envisioned as good only insofar as it brings about a further good (McKenna 2019; note that in his view the good of the harm is still relational since it is dependent on the moral relation between the wrongdoer and the blamer; cf. Bennett 2002).

We contend that the intuition that wrongdoers deserve to be punished frequently involves the notion of basic desert. This claim might be supported by a type of thought experiment about punishment that derives from Immanuel Kant (1797/2017), in which there is no instrumental good to which punishing a wrongdoer would contribute. Imagine that a person on an isolated island viciously murders everyone else on the island and that he is not capable of moral reform due to ingrained hatred and rage. Thus, there are no good consequences that the punishment might aim to realize, and there is no longer a society on the island whose rules might be determined by contract. Many (but not all) nonetheless have the intuition that this murderer deserves to be punished severely. The desert would be basic since the specifics of the example eliminate non-basic desert. Everyday instances of blame also often express the intuition of basic desert. For instance, we may want to blame someone *just because* of what they did and how they were when they did it – i.e., what they knew, what control they had, etc. – and *not* merely because our response may have good consequences or because they have consented to certain norms in advance (Pereboom 2021b, 2022).

As we've noted earlier, basic desert moral responsibility contrasts with a non-basic desert counterpart, which invokes further goods, such as good consequences, to justify desert claims. To explain further, John Rawls (1955) sets out a two-tiered theory in which lawyers, judges, and juries appeal only to backward-looking reasons for punishment, while the practice itself is justified on forward-looking, utilitarian grounds (cf. Hart 1968). In a similar vein, Daniel Dennett (1984, 2003; Dennett in Dennett and Caruso 2021) and Manuel Vargas (2013, 2015) advocate views on which justifications for blame and punishment in our practice of holding morally responsible appeal to claims about what wrongdoers deserve, while that desert is not basic since at a higher level that practice is justified by anticipated good consequences, such as safety and moral reform. On the accounts developed by Dennett and Vargas, our practice of holding agents morally responsible in a desert sense should be retained because doing so yields the best overall consequences relative to alternative practices (cf. Doris 2015).

Others, such as James Lenman (2006) and Ben Vilhauer (2009b, 2013a, 2013b), ground non-basic desert in social contractualist considerations.

In contrast with views that endorse basic and non-basic desert, there are forward-looking accounts of moral responsibility in which the notion of desert has no essential role. On the forward-looking, non-desert-based account of moral responsibility we endorse in Section 3, when we encounter wrongdoing, it is perfectly legitimate to invoke the answerability sense of responsibility, and ask the agent, "Why did you decide to do that?" or "Do you think it was the right thing to do?" If the reasons given in response to such questions are morally unsatisfactory, we regard it as justified to invite the agent to evaluate critically what their actions indicate about their intentions and character, to demand an apology, or to request reform. Engaging in such interactions is reasonable in light of several forward-looking considerations. A first is the right of those harmed or threatened to protect themselves from immoral behavior and its consequences, thereby securing safety. Second, we might have a stake in reconciliation with the wrongdoer, and calling them to account in this way can function as a step toward realizing this objective. Third, on both a personal and societal level we have an interest in the moral formation of the wrongdoer, and the address described functions as a stage in that process. Lastly, such interactions are also justified by the good of the recovery and restoration of victims harmed by wrongdoing. On this forward-looking account of moral responsibility, then, moral protest and exchange is grounded, not in basic desert, but in forward-looking non-desert-invoking desiderata, such as protection, reconciliation, moral formation, and recovery and restoration of victims. Importantly, this account differs from the forward-looking accounts defended by Dennett and Vargas since it does not seek to justify the supposition of desert and associated backward-looking practices.

1.3 Against Consequentialist Accounts of Non-Basic Desert

As we just explained, Daniel Dennett (Dennett and Caruso 2021; cf. Dennett 1984, 2003), Manuel Vargas (2015, cf. 2013), and several other philosophers (McGeer 2015; Sifferd 2021) advocate views according to which the practice-level justifications for blame and punishment invoke backward-looking considerations of desert, while that desert is not basic because at a higher level the practice is justified by anticipated consequences. Dennett maintains that at the practice level our "everyday sense" of desert is preserved:

> The sense of "deserve" that I defend is the everyday sense in which, when you
> win the race fair and square, you deserve the blue ribbon or gold medal; and if
> you wrote the novel, you deserve the royalties, and if you plagiarized it, you

don't; and if you knowingly park in a "No Parking" zone, you deserve a parking ticket; and if you refuse to pay it, you deserve some escalated penalty; and if you committed premeditated murder, you deserve to go to prison for a very long time. (Dennett and Caruso 2021: 18–19)

In the moral responsibility system overall, we need to adopt backward-looking, desert-based practices and policies, yet the system itself is justified on the grounds that it produces the best set of forward-looking outcomes:

> *Of course* it is the "forward-looking benefits" of the *whole system* of desert (praise and blame, reward and punishment) that justifies it, but it justifies the system, while ruling out case-by-case considerations of the specific benefits of lack thereof accruing to any particular instance of blame or punishment. (Dennett in Dennett and Caruso 2021: 18–19; original emphasis)

Some of these beneficial outcomes, according to Dennett, are respect for the law, the effective administration of justice, and proper moral development (Dennett and Caruso 2021).

Vargas's account similarly maintains that preserving the system of desert-based moral responsibility helps cultivate moral agency by fostering and refining the ability to recognize and respond to moral considerations. He calls his account the *agency cultivation account* (Vargas 2013). While conventional accounts evaluate beliefs and practices about blame and praise according to how well they conform to our considered intuitions about basic desert, Vargas's criterion concerns whether the practices "[foster] a distinctive form of agency in us, a kind of agency sensitive to and governed by moral considerations" (Vargas 2013: 173). According to Vargas, moral responsibility is a social practice built upon the responses we have to the ways others treat us, but where the basis for why we ought to continue to participate in practices of praise, blame, and punishment turns, in part, on the effects of these practices upon us as agents.

On Vargas's two-tiered theory, it is our actual practice of holding morally responsible, largely as we now find it, that is justified on forward-looking grounds. The justification functions at the level of practice, by contrast with the level of particular acts. An account of the practice of holding morally responsible that we find in David Hume (1739/1978, 1748/2000) and P. F. Strawson (1962) has it that this practice is a result and expression of a relatively fixed human nature. On this account, it is a salutary practice that regulates our actions, attitudes, and dispositions to the benefit of all. There is room for some change in this practice, but justified change is decidedly limited.

Vargas also endorses the position that this practice more or less as we find it is justified by forward-looking considerations:

> Despite the potentially revisionist nature of this approach – revisionist to the
> extent that the result of prescriptive philosophical theorizing conflicts with
> folk commitments – the project is fundamentally conservative. On this
> approach the main issue is whether our existing practices (or something
> very much like them) are justified, and whether typical judgements of
> moral responsibility are true. (Vargas 2015: 2661–62)

Vargas reluctantly allows for some revision, but not for very much:

> I have argued that the crucial issue is whether there are many, or any cases
> where our practices and judgments are such that [his position] cannot provide
> an adequate normative basis. It is not clear what such a case would be. Yet let
> us suppose that there are some such cases. Perhaps, for example, Texas-style
> death penalty attitudes and practices cannot persist without some form of
> desert that cannot be recast along the two-tiered lines I have endorsed. If so, it
> is difficult to see how these cases would be widespread. (Vargas 2015: 2662)

The two-tiered nature of the position arguably facilitates this conservatism,
because on this conception the practice and its desert presuppositions are relatively insulated from the forward-looking considerations that justify it overall.

Dennett adopts a similar conservatism. While he acknowledges that it
remains an "open empirical question" whether, on balance, we would be better
off without our current moral responsibility system, he thinks it's "not very
open!" (Dennett and Caruso 2021: 26):

> I cannot see how you can think we would be better off without a system of
> desert ... For without my kind of desert, no one would deserve to receive the
> prize they competed for in good faith and won, no one would deserve to be
> blamed for breaking solemn promises without excuse, no one would deserve
> to have their driver's license revoked for drunk driving, no one would deserve
> punishment for lying under oath, and so forth. There would be no rights, no
> recourse to authority or protect against fraud, theft, rape, murder. In short, no
> morality. (Dennett and Caruso 2021: 26)

Dennett goes on to argue that "there is plenty of evidence for a powerful innate
foundation of negative reactions (of anger, of the urge to retaliate ...) when
mammals, especially social mammals, encounter recalcitrant individuals"
(Dennett and Caruso 2021: 46). In his view:

> There are *good* (consequentialist) *reasons* that human cultures have adopted
> largely consensual moralities and raised their offspring to honor them. People
> don't have to reflect on, or even consider, the *free-floating rationales* ... that
> ground their reactive attitudes – people can just take them as part of human
> nature – but they are good design features because they have had good conse-
> quences in the evolutionary past. (Dennett in Dennett and Caruso 2021: 47)

While Dennett acknowledges that with "changing times and changing knowledge, we may decide we want to try to suppress or redirect these very natural reactions" (ibid.), he nevertheless thinks the bulk of our system of desert should be preserved. In particular, "there is still a good case to be made for maintaining the policy that *holds people who have a certain kind of free will responsible*, blaming and punishing them for their transgressions" (Dennett and Caruso 2021: 47).

In Section 4, we'll see how an optimistic skeptic could respond to Dennett's concerns about the implications of basic desert skepticism for rights, morality, and social order. In this section, we focus on three reasons for rejecting two-tiered accounts of moral responsibility along with their inherent conservatism. The first has to do with the free will debate and how best to understand the substantive dispute between the competing leading views. The second concerns the purported benefits of preserving the system of desert. Dennett, for instance, acknowledges that it's an empirical question whether maintaining our desert-based moral responsibility practices is the best way to achieve the forward-looking goals he and Vargas seek. The conservatism of Vargas and Dennett, for instance, is justified only if there is no practice available to us that does substantively better at securing the forward-looking goals. We maintain, however, that there *is a better alternative*: a single-tier forward-looking account like the one we develop in Section 3, one that eschews altogether the notion of desert. Lastly, we reject the conservative assumption about human nature and its lack of malleability and argue instead that human beings are sufficiently malleable for adopting our alternative instead.

Let's begin with the historic free will debate. For reasons we'll explain in the following section, many contemporary philosophers define free will in terms of the control in action required for moral responsibility. Defining free will in this way captures the practical importance of the debate. As Vargas writes:

> One advantage of making explicit an understanding of free will as linked to responsibility, is that it anchors philosophical concerns in something comparatively concrete and undeniably important to our lives. This is not a sense of free will whose only implication is whether it fits with a given philosopher's particular speculative metaphysics. It is not a sense of free will that is arbitrarily attached to a particular religious framework. Instead, it is a notion of free will that understands its significance in light of the role or function it plays in widespread and recognized forms of life. (Vargas 2013: 180)

Linking the notions of free will and moral responsibility fits with our everyday understanding of these conceptions. There is, for instance, growing evidence not only that ordinary people view free will and moral responsibility as intimately tied together but also that it is precisely the desire to blame, punish, and uphold moral responsibility that motivates belief in free will (see, e.g., Clark et al. 2014, 2018; Shariff et al. 2014; Feldman, Wong, and Baumeister 2016; Clark, Winegard, and Baumeister 2019; Everett et al. 2021). People, for instance, attribute more free will to performers of morally bad actions than morally good actions and morally neutral actions (Feldman, Wong, and Baumeister 2016; Clark et al. 2018; Everett et al. 2021), and pondering over morally bad actions leads people to increase their belief in free will of all humankind (Clark et al. 2014). They also appear to understand responsibility for actions and consequences first and foremost in a non-consequentialist sense (Cushman 2008). For instance, empirical findings from Shariff et al. (2014) and others support the hypothesis that free will beliefs, at least among ordinary people, positively predict retributive and backward-looking attitudes (see also Carlsmith and Darley 2008).

But while we agree with Vargas on the link between free will and moral responsibility, we further maintain that it is best to understand the relevant sense of moral responsibility in terms of basic desert, exclusive of non-basic desert (Pereboom 2001, 2014a, 2021a, 2021b, 2022; Caruso 2012, 2021b; Caruso and Morris 2017). This provides a neutral definition of free will, the control in action required for basic desert moral responsibility, that allows for substantive disagreement in the debate. Consider the traditional question concerning the compatibility of free will and determinism. Consequentialist approaches to moral responsibility are forward-looking in the sense that agents are considered proper targets of blame and punishment on the ground that such treatment will reduce the incidence of future immoral behavior. Such approaches include those, such as Vargas's and Dennett's, that ground non-basic desert on consequentialist considerations. However, there is nothing about determinism that challenges the claim that we are morally responsible understood in this consequentialist way. Basic desert-based responsibility, on the other hand, is challenged by determinism (as the manipulation argument makes clear). By defining free will as the control in action required for basic desert moral responsibility, we can formulate the key question in the free will debate as: Do agents have the control in action (i.e., the free will) required to justify basic desert-based judgments, attitudes, and treatment? In short, basic desert moral responsibility is challenged by determinism (and by other potential threats to free will, such as indeterminism), and so it can serve as the focus of the debate.

Some philosophers identify themselves as compatibilists because they hold that some non-basic-desert notion of moral responsibility, often one they regard as sufficient for the moral life, is compatible with determinism

(Jackson 1998; Dennett 2003; Vargas 2007; McGeer 2015). But if "compatibilism" is defined so that such a position turns out to be compatibilist, virtually everyone in the debate stands to be a compatibilist, thus eliminating substantive disagreement about whether compatibilism is true. Frank Jackson says:

> What compatibilist arguments show, or so it seems to me, is not that free action as understood by the folk is compatible with determinism, but that free action on a conception near enough to the folk's to be regarded as a natural extension of it, and which does the theoretical job we folk give the conception of free action in adjudicating questions of moral responsibility and punishment, and in governing our attitudes to the actions of those around us, is compatible with determinism. (1998: 44–45)

Dennett likewise specifies that his compatibilist notion of free will can "play all of the valuable roles free will has been traditionally invoked to play" (2003: 225). But hard determinists such as Spinoza, and hard incompatibilists such as your authors, agree that there are determinism-friendly conceptions near enough to the folk's that allows us to adjudicate the practical questions Jackson has in mind, and, in reference to Dennett's proposal, can adequately play the roles free will has traditionally played. As Stephen Morris points out, Dennett "has defined the conceptions of 'free will' and 'moral responsibility' in such a way to eliminate any substantive differences between the 'compatibilist' position he defends and the hard determinist position that philosophers typically understand as being substantively different from compatibilism" (2009: 69). We agree, and have each made similar objections to such accounts (see Pereboom 2017a, 2021b; Caruso in Dennett and Caruso 2021).

In summary, the compatibilist/incompatibilist terminology should reflect the lines of division in the debate, and thus it would be best to use the term "compatibilism" to designate a view in which an agent's having the sort of free will required for moral responsibility in the basic desert sense is compatible with her actions being causally determined by factors beyond her control. Departing from this characterization stands to undermine the value of the terminology for characterizing core opposing positions.

Our second objection to two-tiered accounts is to challenge the claim that our desert-based moral responsibility practices are the best way to achieve the desired forward-looking goals. Consider, for instance, the angry emotions engaged in our practice of holding people morally responsible. We maintain that such emotions are often destructive, in particular if the forward-looking aims of the practice are not on the minds of the practitioners, but left to a justificatory role at the more abstract second tier (Pereboom 2021a). Consider first how our practice of holding morally responsible malfunctions in personal relationships. Here the practice involves desert-presupposing confrontational moral anger in its resentful and indignant forms. This threat to relationships results from the alienating effect that expressions of such anger have on others, and from such anger's propensity to give rise to defensive or offensive reactions rather than reform and reconciliation. It's clear that expressing anger often has the result of alienating its target and undermining relationships. For example, parents' tendency to react angrily and without concern for compassion to their teenage children's misbehavior can seriously impair their relationship with them, and result in the teen's damaging behavior.

Consider also how our practice of holding morally responsible malfunctions in societal relationships. The political conversation often features accusation and blame not intended to reform and reconcile, but to defeat and disempower. A reason why the practice malfunctions in personal and societal relationships is that the emotions it recruits are in tension with other requirements for the stability of these relationships (Pereboom 2021a). In circumstances of conflict, this requires that participants believe the truth concerning the pertinent emotional attitudes and behavior of others, and that the attitudes of the participants be conciliatory and compassionate. But as Hannah Pickard (2013) points out, anger that accompanies blame has a strong tendency to distort judgments of blameworthiness. Studies by Mark Alicke and his associates indicate that subjects who evaluate the actions of others unfavorably and blame them as a result readily exaggerate the putative wrongdoer's causal control and the evidence that might favor it, while at the same time discounting the counterevidence (Alicke 2000; Alicke, Rose, and Bloom 2012). Alicke calls this tendency *blame validation*. Evidence that blaming behavior is widely subject to problems of these kinds is mounting (Nadelhoffer 2006). Furthermore, as Austin Duggan (2020) argues, there is reason to believe that the anger accompanying blame is the factor that produces these consequences. Studies show that anger degrades reasoning processes in multiple respects (Lerner, Goldberg, and Tetlock 1998; Goldberg, Lerner, and Tetlock 1999; Litvak et al. 2010). Anger results in a proclivity to overlook circumstances that would mitigate blame; it enhances the disposition to view ambiguous behavior as hostile, strengthens the tendency to rely on stereotypes about irrelevant features such as race and ethnicity, and heightens the likelihood of discounting the role of uncontrollable factors in assessing responsibility of wrongdoing. In one study, Julie Goldberg and her associates discovered that when retributive desires to inflict pain or harm are unsatisfied, anger "activate[s] an indiscriminate tendency to punish others in unrelated situations without regard for whether their actions were intentional" (Goldberg, Lerner, and Tetlock 1999: 783).

Our last objection has to do with the practice-level conservatism of the two-tiered approach. Absolute inflexibility about the practice of holding people morally responsible is implausible, even if conceived as a resolutely backward-looking, basic-desert-invoking conception, since it's not credible that the current practice is accurate in its implementation of basic-desert justifications. Moreover, virtually everyone agrees that the practice of a thousand years ago has been revised for the better at least in some respects – that we, for example, no longer use trial by ordeal as a method for determining wrongdoing counts as progress. And if progress has been made in the past, why not now? On the other hand, in arguing for conservatism Vargas and Dennett can't merely be endorsing a version of the practice that is ideal in the sense that all parties, given adequate rationality and information, would agree that it needs no revision.

Conservatism about the practice so conceived isn't a substantive thesis in this context, and we should take them as making a substantive claim. However, it's not evident exactly how conservative they want to be, and so we will focus our critique not on what they actually maintain, but on a resolute conservatism abstracted from any specific theorist, the proponent of which we will call "the conservative."

The conservative endorses a two-level view on which a practice of holding morally responsible that does not differ significantly from our actual practice is best, relative to substantially revised versions of the practice, at realizing human flourishing. Such revised practices would do worse, at least in part because human nature does not allow for serious changes that are not damaging to human flourishing overall.

Such a position is reflected in P.F. Strawson's (1962) claim that the reactive attitudes that form the core of our practice of holding morally responsible, such as resentment, indignation, and guilt, express our human nature, and substantial revisions of that practice would lead to an objectivity of attitude that would jeopardize the value of the relationships that make our lives meaningful.

In favor of conservatism one might argue that aspects of human nature engaged in the practice of holding morally responsible, such as the emotional disposition manifested in blaming and praising, are largely fixed and unmalleable. Against this, we can turn to cross-cultural differences in the emotions invoked in moral practice (see, also, Flanagan 2019, 2021; Pereboom 2021a, 2021b). In their survey of a broad range of anthropological research on emotional regulation, Jozefien De Leersnyder, Michael Boiger, and Batja Mesquita (2013) report, first, that in European and American contexts, good relationships are generally conceived as those in which each partner remains autonomous and partners mutually strengthen each other's individuality and independence.

These characteristics are reinforced by partners in relationships focusing on the positive characteristics that show each partner's uniqueness and that enable them to be self-reliant. Constructive conflict is regarded as necessary for strong relational ties. Emotions such as pride and anger are viewed as reflecting individual self-worth and personal autonomy. By contrast, in most East Asian contexts, partners in relationships generally function as more interdependent and interconnected and more readily adjust to each other's expectations. Emotions such as shame and guilt appear to be conducive to building strong relationships since they promote alignment with social rules and relational embeddedness. Anger appears to be highly undesirable because it threatens relational harmony.

For a more marked contrast, De Leersnyder, Boiger, and Mesquita (2013) cite anthropologist Jean Briggs's (1970) study of the Utkuhiksalingmiut Inuit of Canada's Nunavut territory who rarely express anger. While infants display the characteristic outbursts of negative emotion, children are educated by role modeling and calm guidance to avoid it. In Briggs's analysis, the group's closeness and harmony is the cultural goal that underlies this practice. For De Leersnyder et al., these examples illustrate the phenomenon of cultural regulation of the emotions, which they understand as processes that result in alignment of emotions with cultural values, ideals, goals, and concerns. In their assessment, cultures vary significantly in how they regulate emotions, and indeed, the variations just cited attest to considerable human flexibility regarding the emotions engaged in holding morally responsible (Pereboom 2021b).

We have evidence, then, that features of human nature at work in the practice of holding morally responsible are revisable, and that certain aspects of the practice are credibly at odds with human flourishing. Can we put the two together: are serious revisions possible that would promote human flourishing? The answer, we contend, is a resounding yes. In fact, this has already happened over the past half century. Not long ago it was widely held to be legitimate to blame people for being depressed, and for being mentally ill more generally, and in particular for behavior that manifests mental illness; for teachers to express rage in the classroom and to beat their pupils; for criminals to be severely harmed, physically and mentally, in ways not justified by their sentences, by prison guards or by other prisoners. We have made serious inroads against these aspects of the practice, all of which involve recruitment of angry emotions for the domination of specific individuals and groups. The changes are salutary, and the practice is this seriously revisable for the better.

A further way the practice might be revised concerns blame for having what are considered to be immoral political and social views. In view of the corrosive political divisions we currently find, we might ask whether angry blame for holding positions we consider to be morally wrong is the best way forward.

Given the deep divisions, and how easy it is to communicate angry blame over social media, this issue is especially pressing. There is good empirical justification for significant reduction of angry blame targeted at those who espouse opposing values, and for replacing it with an approach that has a better chance of success. In view of the threat to our societies these divisions pose, many recent studies in social psychology have addressed this issue. For instance, Fieke Harinck and Gerben Van Kleef (2012) argue, on the basis of several studies, that while at least in the short term anger is effective in conflicts about interests, it is not effective in conflicts about values. In conflicts closely tied to a person's values, norms and identity, expressions of anger occasion *the backfire effect*, that is, an outcome in which beliefs and dispositions to act targeted for revision are strengthened and not weakened by the interaction (Nyhan and Reifler 2010, 2015). Their studies provide evidence that people regard expressions of anger as more unfair in value conflicts than in interest conflicts, and that we are more likely to engage retaliatory and escalatory behavior when confronted with angry attempted refutation in a value conflict. Angry blame may be effective in calling attention to wrongdoing and in communicating its effect on its victims. But studies show, and we have reason from experience to believe, that when strongly held values are confronted, an approach different from angry blame is best adopted instead, one that addresses these values by understanding their nature and motivation, and using this knowledge to implement sympathetic ways to realize constructive modification (Trevors et al. 2016; Pereboom 2021a).

We maintain that while empirical questions about the effectiveness of different forward-looking versions of the practice of holding morally responsible are unresolved, the practice shows more malleability than Strawsonians concede – which should be kept in mind when formulating proposals for such forward-looking accounts. In Section 3 we will set out a version on which our ground-level practice of holding morally responsible is directly sensitive to forward-looking aims such as moral formation and reconciliation and is not subject to a barrier between tiers. We'll argue that on this proposal, forward-looking considerations can more readily motivate substantial revisions, notably to the aspects of our practice engaged to disempower and dominate others, and which enlist the angry emotions to advance that objective. If we are correct, then the conservatism of Vargas and Dennett is unjustified and there are, in fact, alternatives to our current system of desert that better serve human well-being.

2 Skepticism about Basic Desert

In this section, we examine the central arguments for skepticism about basic desert. These arguments aim to justify the claim that for an agent to basically deserve the pain or harm of blame or punishment, they must have a kind of control in action – i.e., free will – that is unavailable to us (see, e.g., Strawson 1986; Pereboom 1995, 2001, 2014a, 2021b; Levy 2011; Waller 2011; Caruso 2012, 2021b).

2.1 Free Will and Moral Responsibility

Historically, debates about moral responsibility have been intimately connected with the traditional free will debate. This is because, for an agent to be morally responsible for their action – i.e., to justly deserve to be praised and blamed, punished and rewarded for it – it is typically held that they need to satisfy two individually necessary and jointly sufficient conditions: an *epistemic condition* and a *control condition*. The first condition is concerned with whether the agent's epistemic or cognitive state was such that they can properly be held accountable for the action and its consequences (Rudy-Hiller 2018). The second condition has to do with whether the agent possessed an adequate degree of control in performing the action. Whereas the first condition prompts us to ask, "was this person *aware* of what they were doing (of its consequences, moral significance, etc.)?" the second condition prompts us to ask, "was this person acting *freely* when they did *A*?" (Rudy-Hiller 2018). It is this second condition, the control condition, that philosophers typically associate with free will.

We follow tradition and define "free will" as an agent's ability to exercise the control in acting required to be morally responsible for an action – see, e.g., Pereboom (2001, 2014a), Strawson (1986, 1994), O'Connor (2000), Mele (2006), McKenna (2008), Campbell (1957), Clarke (2005), Levy (2011), Richards (2000), van Inwagen (1983), Wolf (2011), Caruso (2012, 2021b), Morris (2015), Vargas (2007), Nahmias (2014), Dennett (1984), Dennett and Caruso (2021), and Talbert (2016) – though we further specify that the kind of moral responsibility at issue in the traditional free will debate is basic desert moral responsibility. We contend that this definition best serves to draw clear lines of difference between the disputing parties and captures what has been of central philosophical and practical importance in the debate. Since we understand free will as the control in action required for true attributions of basic desert, if the skeptical arguments against free will discussed in this section succeed, they also establish a skepticism about basic desert moral responsibility.

2.2 The Problem of Free Will: Positions and Background

Contemporary theories of free will can be divided into one of two general categories, namely, those that insist on and those that are skeptical about the reality of free will and basic desert moral responsibility. The former category includes *libertarian* and *compatibilist* accounts of free will, two general views that defend the claim that we have free will but disagree on its nature or its conditions. The second category comprises a family of skeptical views that doubt or deny human free will. The main dividing line between the two pro–free will positions, libertarianism and compatibilism, is best understood in terms of the traditional problem of free will and determinism. *Determinism*, as it is commonly understood, is the thesis that at any given time only one future is physically possible (van Inwagen 1983: 3). Or put differently, it is the thesis that facts about the remote past in conjunction with the laws of nature entail that there is only one unique future (McKenna and Pereboom 2016: 19). The traditional problem of free will and determinism therefore comes in trying to reconcile our intuitive sense of free will with the idea that our choices and actions may be causally determined by factors over which we have no ultimate control, that is, the past before we were born and the laws of nature.

Libertarians and compatibilists react to this problem in different ways. *Libertarians* acknowledge that if determinism is true, and all of our actions are causally determined by antecedent circumstances, we lack free will and moral responsibility. Yet they further maintain that at least some of our choices and actions must be free in the sense that they are not causally determined. Libertarians therefore reject causal determinism and defend an indeterminist conception of free will in order to save what they maintain are necessary conditions for free will – that is, the *ability to do otherwise* in exactly the same set of conditions and/or the idea that we remain, in some important sense, the *ultimate source/originator* of action.

Compatibilists, on the other hand, set out to defend a conception of free will that can be reconciled with determinism. They hold that what is of utmost importance is not the absence of causal determination, but that our actions are voluntary, free from constraint and compulsion, and caused in the appropriate way. Different compatibilist accounts spell out requirements for free will differently but widely endorsed views single out responsiveness to reasons or connection of action to what one would reflectively endorse.

Free will skepticism stands in contrast to these pro–free will positions since it takes seriously the possibility that human beings are never morally responsible in the basic desert sense. In the past, the leading form of skepticism was *hard determinism*: the view that determinism is true and incompatible with free will – either because it precludes the ability to do otherwise (*leeway incompatibilism*) or because it is inconsistent with one's being the ultimate source of action (*source incompatibilism*) – hence, no free will. For hard determinists, libertarian free will is an impossibility because human actions are part of a fully deterministic world and compatibilism is operating in bad faith. The hard determinist invokes the naturalistic consideration that everything that happens, including all of our actions, is made inevitable by the remote past physical events together with the laws of nature. It maintains that human beings are situated in a natural world of law-governed causes and effects, and as a result our character and actions are conditioned by causes that we do not control, including our genetic make-up, our upbringing, and the physical environment. Because of these general features of the universe, the hard determinist maintains that we cannot have the sort of control in action required for basic desert attributions

While hard determinism had its classic statement in the time when Newtonian physics reigned, it has very few defenders today – largely because the development of quantum mechanics diminished confidence in determinism, for the reason that it has indeterministic interpretations. This is not to say that determinism has been refuted or falsified by modern physics, because it has not. In fact, a number of leading interpretations of quantum mechanics are consistent with determinism (see e.g., Bohm 1952; Vaidman 2014; Lewis 2016). It is also important to keep in mind that even if we allow some indeterminacy to exist at the microlevel of the universe, the level studied by quantum mechanics, there may still remain determinism-where-it-matters – that is, at the ordinary level of choices and actions, and even the electrochemical activity in our brains (Honderich 2002: 5).

Most contemporary free will skeptics, however, now offer arguments that are agnostic about determinism. For instance, some free will skeptics argue that free will is in fact impossible independently of the truth of determinism. Most prominently, Galen Strawson contends in his Basic Argument that *ultimate responsibility*, that is, moral responsibility in the basic desert sense, requires a type of agency that human beings cannot have, and its impossibility for us can be established independently of the truth (or falsity) of causal determinism (Strawson 1986: 25–60, 1994). The core idea of the Basic Argument can be expressed as follows. When an agent acts, she acts because of the way she is. But to be ultimately responsible for her action, she must then be ultimately responsible for the way she is, at least in the salient mental respects. But if she is to be ultimately responsible for how she is in those mental respects, she must be ultimately responsible for the way she is that resulted in those mental respects. This reasoning generates a regress, which indicates that finite beings like us can never satisfy the conditions of ultimate responsibility. The conclusion is that finite agents like us can never be ultimately responsible for any of their actions.

Randolph Clarke (2005) contests Strawson's supposition that ultimate responsibility requires that the agent be in rational control of all there was about her, mentally speaking, that causally brought it about that she acted as she did. Imagine that we're created with agent-causal libertarian powers and pre-programmed with a set of strong self-interested reasons and a set of roughly equally strong altruistic reasons but no reasons for action of other kinds (e.g., to do evil for evil's sake). We would then not be ultimately responsible for the fact that our actions are all either self-interested or altruistic. However, despite this, when it's up to an agent to select either a self-interested option or an altruistic one and she selects the altruistic one, it would seem that she can still be ultimately responsible for selecting the altruistic option rather than the self-interested one. Clarke's criticism of the Basic Argument may indicate that the standard for rational control this argument assumes is too stringent. We think that Clarke may be right about this.

Another argument for free will skepticism maintains that regardless of the causal structure of the universe, free will and basic desert moral responsibility are incompatible with the pervasiveness of *luck* (see, e.g., Levy 2009, 2011; Caruso 2019a, 2021b). Consider, for instance, the significant role luck plays in our lives. First, there is the initial "lottery of life" or "luck of the draw," over which we have no say. Whether we are born into poverty or affluence, war or peace, abusive or loving homes, is simply a matter of luck. It is also a matter of luck what natural gifts, talents, predispositions, and physical traits we were born with.

Beyond this initial lottery of life, there is also the luck of what breaks one encounters during one's period of self-formation and what environmental influences are most salient on us. Combined, these matters of luck determine what Thomas Nagel famously calls *constitutive luck* – luck in who one is and what character traits and dispositions one has. Many philosophers think constitutive luck creates a problem for basic desert moral responsibility. The concern is that, since our genes, parents, peers, and other environmental influences all contribute to making us who we are, and since we have no control over these, it seems that who we are is at least largely a matter of luck. And since how we act is partly a function of who we are, the existence of constitutive luck entails that what actions we perform depends on luck (Nelkin 2004/2013).

Neil Levy (2011) develops this concern further by arguing that the pervasiveness of constitutive luck, along with a second kind of luck, *present luck*, completely undermine free will and moral responsibility. Whereas constitutive luck is the luck that causes relevant properties of agents, such as their desires, beliefs, dispositions, and character traits, *present luck* (Mele 2006; Levy 2011) is the luck at or around the moment of a putatively free and morally responsible action or decision. Present luck may include any genuine indeterminism that may exist in the proximal causal chain leading to action, as libertarians posit, as well as any circumstantial or situational influences that may affect an agent's choice or action in a way that is outside their control. It can also include features of what Heather Gert (2018) calls *awareness luck* – luck in how aware we are of the morally significant features of our surroundings. At the heart of Levy's argument is the following dilemma, which he calls the *luck pincer*: either actions are subject to present luck, or they are subject to constitutive luck, or both. Either way, luck undermines moral responsibility since it undermines responsibility-level control.

Consider, for instance, how this argument would work against certain forms of compatibilism. A historical compatibilist could respond to the luck pincer by claiming that as long as an agent takes responsibility for their endowments, dispositions, and values, over time they will become morally responsible for them. The problem with this reply is that the series of actions through which agents shape and modify their endowments, dispositions, and values are themselves significantly subject to either present luck or constitutive luck – and, as Levy puts it, "we cannot undo the effects of luck with more luck" (2009: 244). Hence, the very actions to which history-sensitive compatibilists point, the actions whereby agents take responsibility for their endowments, either express that endowment (when they are explained by constitutive luck) or reflect the agent's present luck, or both (see Levy 2009: 247, 2011).

Hence, the luck pincer.

In addition to the Basic Argument and the luck pincer, there is yet another route to free will skepticism – i.e., the one we have argued for elsewhere (see Pereboom 2001, 2014a, 2022; Caruso 2012, 2021b). Like the hard determinist, it maintains that we do not have the kind of free will needed for basic desert moral responsibility. But this is not because it assumes the truth of determinism, and that all of our actions are causally determined by preceding factors beyond our control, although this may well be true. Instead, it argues that any sort of indeterminism that has a good chance of being true is also incompatible with free will in the sense just defined. A more accurate name for our position would therefore be *hard incompatibilism* (Pereboom 2001, 2014a), to differentiate it from hard determinism.

Hard incompatibilism amounts to a rejection of both compatibilism and libertarianism. It maintains that the sort of free will required for basic desert moral responsibility is incompatible with causal determination by factors beyond the agent's control and *also* with the kind of indeterminacy in action required by the most plausible versions of libertarianism. We contend that the most direct and convincing route to this conclusion runs as follows. Against the view that free will is compatible with the causal determination of our actions by natural factors beyond our control, we argue that there is no relevant difference between this prospect and our actions being causally determined by manipulators. Against event causal libertarianism, we advance the disappearing agent objection, according to which agents are left unable to settle whether a decision occurs and hence cannot have the control required for moral responsibility. The same problem, we contend, arises for noncausal libertarian accounts, which also fail to provide agents with the control in action required for basic desert moral responsibility. While agent-causal libertarianism could, in theory, supply this sort of control, we argue that it cannot be reconciled with our best physical theories and faces additional problems accounting for mental causation. Since this exhausts the options for views on which we have the sort of free will at issue, we conclude that free will skepticism is the only remaining position (see Pereboom 2001, 2014a; Caruso 2012, 2021b). To these arguments we now turn.

2.3 The Manipulation Argument against Compatibilism

Compatibilists maintain that even if all of our actions are causally determined by factors beyond our control, we can still have the free will, the control in action, required to be morally responsible in the basic desert sense for them. Compatibilists of this kind point out that causal determination is irrelevant to the commonplace criteria we use to ascertain whether people are blameworthy. In legal cases defense attorneys may want to establish that the accused was not compelled by someone else to commit the crime, and that he was rational when he acted. Whether causal determinism is true, compatibilists contend, is not relevant to whether people are compelled or irrational, and moreover and more generally, whether determinism is true is never a consideration in court cases. Compatibilists set out conditions for moral responsibility that do not require the falsity of determinism, and they argue that satisfying such compatibilist conditions is sufficient for responsibility. Incompatibilists object that even if someone satisfies these compatibilists conditions, being causally determined by factors beyond her control rules out moral responsibility in the sense at issue. Does this amount to a standoff, or can progress be made in this discussion?

The best way to argue against the compatibilist option, in our view, starts with the intuition that in a case in which an agent is intentionally causally determined to act by, for example, neuroscientists who manipulate her brain by optogenetic stimulation, she will not be morally responsible for that action in the basic desert sense even if the compatibilist conditions are met. Next, we point out that there are no differences relevant to basic desert moral responsibility between this case and a possible case that features an agent who is causally determined to act in an ordinary naturalistic way. The conclusion is that an agent is not morally responsible in the basic desert sense if she is causally determined to act by factors beyond her control even if she satisfies the compatibilist conditions (Taylor 1974: 45; Pereboom 1995: 22–26, 2001: 110–20, 2014a: 71–103; Kane 1996: 65–69; Mele 2006: 186–94).

In the four-case version of this argument (Pereboom 1995, 2001: 110–27, 2014a: 71–103), in each of four cases an agent commits a crime, murder, for self-interested reasons. All of the cases are designed so that the action conforms to the compatibilist conditions. For instance, the action meets a criterion advocated by David Hume (1739/1978): the agent is not compelled to act by other agents or constrained by other factors such as drugs. The action also meets the rationality condition advocated by John Fischer (1994; Fischer and Ravizza 1998): the agent's desires can be modified by, and some of them arise from, his rational consideration of his reasons, and if he understood that the bad consequences for himself that would result from the crime would be much more severe than they are actually likely to be, he would have refrained from the crime for that reason. Finally, the action meets the compatibilist condition proposed by Harry Frankfurt (1971): the agent's effective desire (i.e., their will) conforms appropriately to their second-order desire for which effective desire they will have.

The manipulation cases serve to indicate that it's possible for an agent who knowingly acts wrongly to be morally non-responsible in the basic desert sense even if the compatibilist conditions are satisfied, and that, as a result, these conditions are insufficient for such moral responsibility, contrary to what the compatibilist claims. The argument adds force by setting out three such manipulation cases, each of which is progressively more like a fourth, in which the action is causally determined in an ordinary and natural way. These cases are designed with the aim that there be no difference relevant to basic desert moral responsibility between any two adjacent cases. Thus if it's agreed that the agent isn't morally responsible in the first case, this feature of the argument will make it difficult to affirm that he is responsible in the final, ordinary case:

> Case 1: A team of neuroscientists possesses the technology and skill to manipulate Professor Plum's neural states remotely. In this particular case, they do so by pressing a button just before he begins to reason about his situation, which they know will result in a neural state that realizes a strongly egoistic reasoning process, which the neuroscientists know will deterministically result in his decision to kill White. Plum would not have killed White had

the neuroscientists not intervened, because his reasoning would then not have been sufficiently egoistic to produce the decision to kill.

Case 2: Plum is just like an ordinary human being, except that a team of neuroscientists has programmed him at the beginning of his life so that his reasoning is often but not always egoistic, and at times strongly so, with the intended consequence that in his current circumstances he will be causally determined to engage in the process of deliberation that results in his decision to kill White for egoistic reasons.

Case 3: Plum is an ordinary human being, except that the training practices of his community causally determined the nature of his deliberative reasoning processes so that they are often but not always egoistic. On this occasion, his deliberative process is exactly as it is in Cases 1 and 2: in his current circumstances he is causally determined to engage in the process of deliberation that results in his decision to kill White for egoistic reasons.

Case 4: All that occurs in our universe is causally determined by virtue of its past states together with the laws of nature. Plum is an ordinary human being, raised in normal circumstances, but his reasoning processes are frequently but not exclusively egoistic, and sometimes strongly so. In the current circumstances he is causally determined to engage in the process of deliberation that results in his decision to kill White, for egoistic reasons.

Case 1 features intentional, causally determining manipulation that is local in the sense that it takes place close to the time of the action. Of the four cases it is the one that most reliably elicits an immediate non-responsibility intuition. Case 2 is like Case 1, except that it restricts the deterministic manipulation to the beginning of Plum's life, and so with respect to Plum's action it is not local and is more remote. Case 3 is distinctive in that the deterministic manipulation results from community upbringing. Case 4 is the ordinary deterministic case in which the causal determination of Plum's action is not intentional, but results from the past and the laws of nature. Case 4 is a standard kind of case about which compatibilists claim that the agent is morally responsible despite being causally determined to act by factors beyond his control.

In Case 1, might Plum be basic-desert morally responsible for his action? It seems intuitive that Plum is a causally determined victim of conniving neuroscientists, and not morally responsible in the basic desert sense. Are there responsibility-relevant differences, then, between Cases 1 and 2 that would justify the verdict that he is not morally responsible in Case 1 but is morally responsible in Case 2? We maintain that there are not. Note, the aim was to construct the four cases so that it isn't possible to draw a difference relevant to the type of moral responsibility at issue between any two adjacent cases. Supposing this absence of relevant differences, if Plum is not responsible in Case 1, he isn't responsible in Cases 2, 3, and 4 either. We contend that the unifying best explanation for Plum's non-responsibility in the four cases is that in each he is causally determined to act by factors beyond his control. Hence the argument's anti-compatibilist conclusion.

Compatibilists, in turn, respond to this argument by adopting either *hard-line* or *soft-line* replies (McKenna 2008). Hard-line replies insist that Plum is morally responsible in all four cases, or at the very least that it is not clear that Plum is not responsible in these cases, while a soft-line reply claims that he is responsible in some of the cases although not in others. Hard-liners grant that there is no relevant difference between agents in the various manipulated scenarios and ordinary (non-manipulated) agents in deterministic settings; instead they attack the intuition that agents are not morally responsible in the manipulated cases. They maintain that as long as the various compatibilist conditions for moral responsibility are satisfied, manipulated agents are just as free and morally responsible as determined agents – despite what might be our initial intuition. Soft-line replies, on the other hand, try to differentiate between the various cases. They search for relevant differences between the cases, differences that would account for why manipulated agents are not free and morally responsible, but non-manipulated and causally determined agents are. There are, however, problems with both types of replies.

The first problem with the hard-line approach is that it conflicts too deeply with our intuitions about sourcehood and the relevant class of manipulation cases. Many people find it highly implausible that Plum, in Case 1, could be morally responsible in the basic desert sense for his behavior given how the behavior came about. And it is not just a matter of intuition that leads us to conclude this. The incompatibilist can argue that whatever sourcehood is at the end of the day, Plum (in Case 1) clearly doesn't have it. And since sourcehood is required for basic desert moral responsibility, we must conclude that Plum is not morally responsible (see Tognazzini 2014).

The second problem with the hard-line approach has to do with the *initial attitude* it adopts toward Case 4, the case of natural determinism, and how it proceeds to argue in the opposite direction that manipulation cases are no threat to free will and moral responsibility. Consider, for instance, the *resolute compatibilist* who adopts an unapologetic hard-line approach that maintains that Plum is morally responsible in all four cases. The problem with this approach is that any arguments for Plum's responsibility in Case 1 will have to overcome the initial intuition that extreme, covert manipulation threatens moral responsibility. Furthermore, this approach would not only require casting doubt on Plum's nonresponsibility, but it must make a strong enough case that inclines us toward Plum's being responsible. But how can the hard-liner establish or show that Plum is responsible in Case 1? What kind of argument can they provide? It would not help to reason in the opposite direction, as hard-liners do, and argue that *since Plum is morally responsible in Case 4* (the case of natural determinism), Plum's responsibility must transfer to Case 1 since there is no relevant difference between agents in Cases 4 and 3, 3 and 2, and 2 and 1. This would be question-begging. Since the responsibility or nonresponsibility of an ordinary determined agent is exactly what is at issue, it cannot be claimed or assumed that Plum in Case 4 is morally responsible.

We maintain that while there are a number of different initial attitudes one can bring to the ordinary deterministic example, the most appropriate attitude to adopt is the *neutral inquiring attitude*. On this attitude, it is initially epistemically rational not to believe that the agent in an ordinary deterministic example is morally responsible in the basic desert sense, and not to believe that he isn't, but to be open to clarifying considerations that would make one or other of these beliefs rational. The reason the neutral inquiring attitude is the appropriate attitude to adopt is that it allows for clarifying considerations to alter our thinking and it's the best one for the opposing parties in the debate to make if there is to be a productive engagement. But once we adopt the neutral inquiring attitude, we can see how an analogous manipulation case functions as a clarifying consideration that makes rational the belief that the ordinary causally determined agent is not morally responsible. The neutral inquiring response – the most epistemically rational attitude to adopt – is open to the potential rational influence of manipulation examples, and so we cannot assume that it transfers to the manipulation cases unaltered. If we adopt the neutral inquiring attitude, manipulation cases, like Cases 1–3, can then be used to clarify our intuitions in a situation where it is clear that an agent's inner psychological states are causally determined by factors beyond their control (i.e., a team of external manipulators), and we can then use those clarifying considerations to inform our thinking in the ordinary deterministic case. Once we adopt the neutral inquiring attitude, manipulation cases can function as a clarifying consideration that makes rational the belief that the naturally determined agent is not morally responsible.

What, then, of soft-line replies? Well, unlike the previous approach, the challenge here is to point to a difference between two adjacent cases that can explain in a principled way why Plum is not morally responsible in the former case but is in the latter. The main problem with the soft-line approach, however, is that any difference identified as the relevant one between manipulated agents and ordinary determined agents may be a difference that applies only to current manipulation cases but not future cases. A number of leading soft-line replies point, for instance, to responsibility-conferring conditions not specified in a particular manipulation case (Lycan 1987; Baker 2006; Feltz 2013; Murray and Lombrozo 2017). But even if one could point to a relevant difference between an agent in an extant manipulation case and an agent in the naturally determined case, this may only serve as an invitation for proponents of the manipulation argument to revise the vignette on which their argument is based so that the agent now satisfies the relevant condition on which the soft-liner insists (Capes, forthcoming). The challenge, then, for defenders of the soft-line approach is to show that there is some kind of requirement for free action and moral responsibility that can be satisfied by agents in deterministic settings, but which cannot, *even in principle*, be satisfied by agents in manipulation cases. We maintain that this cannot be done. Soft-line replies are therefore unconvincing because, at best, they can only show that *a particular* manipulation example has failed to capture all the relevant compatibilist conditions for moral responsibility, *not* that manipulation arguments fail *tout court*.

Given the issues raised for the hard-line and soft-line replies, manipulation arguments, like the four-case argument, should lead us to conclude that determinism is incompatible with an agent being the *appropriate source* of their actions or controlling them in the right kind of way. We maintain that this conclusion, a form of source incompatibilism, is the only reasonable position to adopt. We therefore conclude that an action is free in the sense required for basic desert moral responsibility only if it is not produced by a deterministic process that traces back to causal factors beyond the agent's control.

2.4 The Disappearing Agent Argument against Event-Causal Libertarianism

Next, the justification for the skeptical position about free will also requires arguing against the competing incompatibilist position, libertarianism. On libertarian views we do have the free will at issue, and required for an action's being freely willed is that it not be causally determined by factors beyond the agent's control. Here we'll examine the two most frequently endorsed kinds of libertarianism: *event-causal libertarianism* and *agent-causal libertarianism*.

On the event-causal libertarian position, actions are caused solely by events, conceived as substances having properties at times, such as Abby wanting at noon today to give Rachel her medicine. For an action to be freely willed, some type of indeterminacy in the production of the action by such events is a key requirement (Kane 1996; Ekstrom 2000, 2019; Balaguer 2010). The view that only events can be causes contrasts with one on which substances, such as atoms, machines, and agents can be causes, and not just events in which they have a part. Those who maintain that only events can be causes do sometimes speak as if substances can be causes, but maintain that when we clarify such speech, we will see that the event-causal view is right. For instance, imagine a car drives through a puddle of water and splashes you. We might say; "The car made you wet!" But more exactly, it's not the car that made you wet, but an event, the car's driving through the puddle at 725 5th Avenue in New York at 2 PM on the 7th of April 2022 that had this effect. By contrast, according to agent-causal libertarianism, free will of the sort at issue is accounted for by agents who, specifically as substances, cause actions without being causally determined to do so. In this position, the causation that produces a free choice is not causation among events involving the agent, but is instead a case of the agent fundamentally as a substance causing a choice (e.g., Clarke 1996; O'Connor 2000).

A perennial objection to event-causal libertarianism is that if actions are undetermined in the way it proposes, agents will not have sufficient control in acting to secure moral responsibility for them. The ancient Epicureans maintained that the universe ultimately consists of atoms and the void, and that if universal causal determinism were true, the atoms would all be falling downward. To account for the interaction of atoms and also free will, they posited random swerves in the otherwise downward paths of atoms (Lucretius 50 BCE/1998). At this point we might ask: could we agents control whether atoms swerve, specifically to the extent required to justify basic desert moral responsibility? Similarly, certain interpretations of quantum mechanics feature indeterministic events, which may be taken to undergird free will. Here again we might ask: could agents control such indeterministic events, in particular to the extent that justifies basic desert moral responsibility?

We embellish this concern in the following way. To be morally responsible in the basic desert sense for an action, it's necessary that the agent have a certain robust kind of control in acting. Given the indeterminism specified by event-causal libertarian position, with the complete causal role of the causally relevant preceding events in place, it remains open whether action occurs. And furthermore, the part the agent plays in the production of the action is exhausted by these agent-involving events. Accordingly, nothing about the agent *settles* whether the action occurs, and this indicates that the agent lacks the control in acting required for the kind of moral responsibility at issue. Because the agent "disappears" at the critical point in the production of the action – at the point at which whether it occurs is to be settled – one of us (Pereboom) has called this the *disappearing agent argument* (Pereboom 2014a: 32–33, 2017b).

The core concern here is that because event-causal libertarian agents lack the power to settle which decision occurs, they lack the role in action necessary to secure the control that basic desert moral responsibility requires. Suppose, for instance, that a decision is made in a deliberative context in which the agent's moral motivations favor deciding to A, her prudential motivations favor her deciding to not-A, and the strength(s) of these motivations are in equipoise. A and non-A are the options she is considering. The potentially causally relevant events, typically belief- or desire-involving events, thus render the occurrence of each of these decisions equiprobable. But then the potentially causally relevant events do not settle which decision occurs, that is, whether the decision to A or the decision to not-A occurs. Since, given event-causal libertarianism, only events are causally relevant, nothing settles which decision occurs. Thus it can't be the agent or anything about the agent that settles which decision occurs, and they therefore lack the control required for moral responsibility for it.

On the account of settling we favor, the ability to settle which option for action occurs is an exercise of control in action with two main characteristics: *determination* and *difference making*. To settle whether to A or B, or equivalently, which of A or B occurs, is to determine which of these options occurs. But there is also more to the notion of settling than determining whether an action or decision to act occurs. Helen Steward (2012), for instance, has argued that settling must also involve difference making – that is, making the difference as to which option for actions occurs. Putting the two suggestions together results in the following characterization: Agents settle which option for action occurs just in case they determine which action occurs, and they make the difference as to which action occurs (Pereboom 2017b). Since event-causal libertarianism rules out this ability to settle which option for action occurs, it is unable to preserve the kind of free will needed for basic desert moral responsibility (Pereboom 2014a, 2017b).

Agent-causal libertarianism offers a remedy for this concern. If agents, as substances, are specified as causes, they can have the role of settling whether the action occurs in such an indeterministic context. While on the event-causal alternative any causes involving agents leave it open whether the action occurs, on the agent-causal view, the agent-as-substance can break the tie, and cause the action (or else refrain from doing so) without being causally determined to do so. More exactly, on agent-causal libertarianism agents possess a distinctive causal power, a power for an agent, fundamentally as a substance to cause an action without being causally determined to do so, and thereby to settle whether an action occurs (agent-causal libertarian views are proposed or defended by Kant 1781/1787/1987; Reid 1788/1983; Chisholm 1964, 1976; Clarke 1993, 1996; O'Connor 2000, 2008; Griffith 2010).

2.5 Is Agent-Causal Libertarianism Reconcilable with Science?

Common to all agent-causal accounts is the belief that an intelligible notion of an agent's causing an event can be given according to which the kind of causation involved is fundamentally distinct from the kind that obtains between events. The traditional notion of event causation assumes that all caused events are caused, either deterministically or indeterministically, by prior events. But instead of appealing to event causation, agent-causal theorists introduce a new type of causation, *agent-causation*, to account for human agency and freedom. According to this notion of agent-causation, it is the agent himself or herself that causes, or initiates, free actions. And the agent, which is the cause of their own free actions, is a *self-determining* being, causally undetermined by antecedent events and conditions.

While agent-causal theorists differ over whether they view all intentional actions as agent-causal in nature or just some intentional actions, they all agree that agent-causation is a necessary condition for an action's being free. The following passage by Richard Taylor does a good job summing up the basic position:

> The only conception of action that accords with our data is one according to which people ... are sometimes, but of course not always, self-determining beings; that is, beings which are sometimes the causes of their own behavior. In the case of an action that is free, it must be such that it is caused by the agent who performs it, but such that no antecedent conditions were sufficient for his performing just that action. In the case of an action that is both free and rational, it must be such that the agent who performed it did so for some reason, but this reason cannot have been the cause of it. (1974: 51)

Roderick Chisholm, another leading defender of agent-causal libertarianism, further elaborates this notion of self-determination when he writes:

> If we are responsible, and if what I have been trying to say [about agent causation] is true, then we have a prerogative which some would attribute only to God: each of us, when we act, is a prime unmoved mover. In doing what we do, we cause certain events to happen and nothing – or no one – causes us to cause those events to happen. (1964: 32)

O'Connor prefers the expression "not wholly moved movers" (2000: 67), but the point is similar: According to agent-causal accounts, the agent (qua substance) must be the cause of their decision or action but themselves not causally necessitated to perform just that action – that is, the agent must be a kind of uncaused cause. This is what separates agent-causal accounts from all other accounts of free will.

A frequently cited objection to agent-causal libertarianism is that it cannot be reconciled with scientific theory. Suppose that science reveals that the physical world is wholly governed by deterministic laws. Given this supposition, agent-causal libertarians may make room for their view by claiming that we agents are non-physical beings, and that this allows us to have the agent-causal power in an otherwise deterministic physical world. But this picture gives rise to a problem. On the path to a bodily movement resulting from an undetermined agent-caused decision, physical changes, for example in the agent's brain, occur. At this point we would expect to encounter divergences from the deterministic laws. Alterations in the brain that result from the causally undetermined decision would themselves not be causally determined, and would not be governed by deterministic laws. The agent-causalist may propose that the physical alterations that result from free decisions just happen to dovetail with what can be predicted on the basis of the deterministic laws, and then no event would occur that diverges from these laws. But this proposal features coincidences too wild to be credible. So it appears that agent-causal libertarianism cannot be reconciled with the physical world's being governed by deterministic laws.

A very similar objection can be set out if the laws of physics are fundamentally probabilistic and not deterministic (see Pereboom 1995: 28–30, 2001: 79–85, 2014a: 65–69). Consider the class of possible human actions each of which has a physical component whose antecedent probability of occurring is approximately 0.32. It would not violate the statistical laws in the sense of being logically incompatible with them if, for a large number of instances, the physical components in this class were not actually realized close to 32 percent of the time. Rather, the force of the statistical law is that for a large number of instances it is correct to expect physical components in this class to be realized close to 32 percent of the time. Are free choices on the agent-causal libertarian model compatible with what the statistical law leads us to expect about them? If agent-causal free action were compatible with what according to the statistical law is overwhelmingly likely, then for a large enough number of instances the possible action in our class would have to be freely chosen close to 32 percent of the time. Then, for a large enough number of instances, the possible actions whose physical components have an antecedent probability of 0.32 would almost certainly be freely chosen close to 32 percent of the time. But if the occurrence of these physical components were settled by the choices of agent-causes, then their actually being chosen close to 32 percent of the time would amount to a coincidence no less wild then the coincidence of possible actions whose physical components have an antecedent probability of about 0.99 being chosen, over a large enough number of instances, close to

99 percent of the time. The proposal that agent-causal free choices do not diverge from what the statistical laws predict for the physical components of our actions would run so sharply counter to what we would expect as to make it incredible.

The agent-causalist may now suggest that free decisions do in fact result in divergences from what we would expect given current theories of the physical laws. On this suggestion, divergences from the deterministic or fundamentally probabilistic laws occur whenever we act freely. An objection to this proposal is that we currently have no evidence that such divergences actually occur. Accordingly, it appears that agent-causal libertarianism is not reconcilable with either deterministic or probabilistic laws of nature, and we have no evidence that divergences from these laws are to be found.

While we take the above consideration regarding the laws of nature to be sufficient for the rejection of agent-causal libertarian accounts, the view faces additional objections as well. Consider, for instance, the problem of mental causation. Agent-causal libertarians must clearly preserve our intuitive sense of mental causation, because on their view, agents, as mental substances, are causes. Furthermore, according to agent-causal libertarianism, we are morally responsible by virtue of such mental substance causation, and moreover, mental causation is required for legal responsibility (cf. Morse 2004, 2016, 2018; Sifferd 2006, 2014). The worry, however, is that the standard versions of agent-causal libertarianism are unable to preserve mental causation.

The standard agent-causal libertarian accounts are not physicalist, viewing the self either as an immaterial substance, such as a Cartesian soul (e.g., Foster 1991; Eccles 1994; Swinburne 1996), or else as a substance with radically emergent causal powers, that is, causal powers not determined by (more basic) physical entities and the physical laws governing them (e.g., Hasker 1990; O'Connor 2000, 2008). A concern for these two positions is that they cannot account for how the agent can cause the physical events they would need to cause, such as neural changes and bodily motions. For these positions would appear to be at odds with *physical causal closure*, the principle that every physical event has a sufficient physical cause, that is, a sufficient cause consisting of solely of physical entities. The problem would result because, if an agent is a non-physical mental substance, either because it is an immaterial substance or because it has radically emergent causal powers, then it could not cause physical events without either a contravention of the causal closure of the physical, or else an implausible causal overdetermination of physical events by physical events and non-physical agent causes (Kim 1999; Pereboom 2001: 69–79; Papineau 2002; Caruso 2012, 2021b). To avoid this dilemma, it would seem that the agent-causalist would be forced to accept forms of physicalism according to which agents are identical to or entirely realized by physical entities (see Caruso 2012, 2021b). But on these options, the independence of the physical laws required for agent-causal libertarianism would be jeopardized.

In summary, then, we maintain that both compatibilist and libertarian accounts do not preserve the control in action required for basic desert moral responsibility. The manipulation argument undermines compatibilism; the disappearing agent argument dislodges event-causal libertarianism; and agent-causal libertarianism is not reconcilable with the laws of nature, while we have no evidence of events not governed by these laws.[2] As a result, we conclude that free will skepticism remains the only reasonable position left standing.

3 Forward-Looking Moral Responsibility

If skeptics reject basic desert moral responsibility for the reasons set out in Section 2, and non-basic desert moral responsibility for the reasons outlined in Section 1, where does that leave them with regard to moral responsibility in general? Below, we outline and defend a forward-looking, single-tier, non-desert-based account of moral responsibility that is perfectly consistent with the rejection of free will and desert-based moral responsibility. On this forward-looking account, moral protest and exchange is grounded, not in desert, but in four forward-looking non-desert-invoking desiderata: protection and safety, reconciliation in relationships, moral formation of wrongdoers, and the recovery and restoration of victims of wrongdoing. Importantly, this account differs from the forward-looking accounts defended by Dennett, Vargas, and others since it does not seek to justify the system of desert or any of its controversial backward-looking practices, nor does it seek to capture the kind of moral responsibility at issue in contemporary debates.

3.1 A Single-Tier Forward-Looking View

The sense of moral responsibility we endorse rejects basic desert and is, by contrast, forward-looking. Holding someone morally responsible involves moral protest in the face of bad behavior, and encouragement in the face of good behavior. Moral protest in this sense does not involve blame that involves pain or harm conceived as a basically deserved response to

---

[2] One view not discussed here is non-causal libertarian account (see Ginet 1997), though we maintain that these too fail to preserve the control in action required for basic desert moral responsibility (see Pereboom 2014a, 2022).

a wrong done. Rather, protest in the face of wrongdoing is morally justified insofar as it can be anticipated to secure forward-looking aims such as protection, reconciliation, and moral formation. Immoral actions are often harmful, and we have a right to protect ourselves and others from those who are disposed to behave harmfully. Furthermore, immoral actions stand to impair relationships, and we have a moral interest in undoing such impairment through reconciliation. Because we value morally good character and actions that accord with it, we also have a stake in the moral formation of character when it is beset by dispositions to misconduct. Lastly, we also have an interest in the recovery and restoration of victims harmed by wrongdoing. On some conceptions, this is secured in part by the wrongdoer being punished on grounds of basic desert. But instead, it might be secured instead by apology and compensation upon recognition of wrongdoing and sincere contrition (Pereboom 2017c, 2021b: 36).

The forward-looking position we endorse is a single-tiered view, and it does not feature the notion of desert, whether it be basic or non-basic. We largely endorse Michael McKenna's (2012: 92–94) communicative conception of moral responsibility, with the main revision being the retraction of desert, resentment, and indignation. In his *conversational* theory, actions of a morally responsible agent are potential bearers of a type of meaning by indicating the quality of will the action manifests. Blaming an agent who manifests an immoral quality of will in action is an expression of an attitude such as resentment or indignation, and its goal is to communicate to them a moral response to the quality of will the action indicates. Morally responsible agents understand that other members of the moral community are apt to attribute this type of meaning to their actions. When their actions are morally charged, they understand themselves to be introducing such a meaningful contribution to a conversational exchange. McKenna labels this initial stage of the conversation *moral contribution*, which features actions that are potentially blameworthy or praiseworthy. In the second stage, in the case of apparent wrongdoing the agent is blamed by a respondent. McKenna calls this stage *moral address*. In the third stage, *moral account*, the blamed agent may offer an excuse, a justification, or an apology. The respondent might at this point continue the conversation by forgiving or punishing the wrongdoer. In a subsequent stage the blamed agent may be restored to full status in the moral community.

Our revision of this account has it that those who blame or morally protest wrongdoers have forward-looking considerations such as moral formation and reconciliation as their explicit aims, and that they do not endorse blame as featuring intentional infliction of pain or harm conceived as basically deserved.

To blame may be painful for the wrongdoer, as in McKenna's version – i.e., being called out for having done wrong may be painful, and one may experience the pain or regret as a result (Pereboom 2017c, 2021b).

However, on our account the pain of blaming or protest is not conceived by the blamer as a non-instrumental good imposed in blaming, but rather as an instrumental good in the service of the forward-looking goals to be secured by blaming. Similarly, one who rejects basically deserved pleasure and benefit might also adopt a forward-looking conversational account of praise, where praise has the function of strengthening motivations to act well, and, as Daniel Telech (2021) proposes, to facilitate praiser and praiseworthy agent's recognition of one another as standing for a common value. On the conversational model we endorse, as in McKenna's, the agent's responsiveness to reasons is engaged in the process of blaming (or protesting) and praising (or approving/ encouraging). Focusing on blame, it qualifies as a mode of communication whose first objective is having a wrongdoer acknowledge that the reasons for which they acted are morally inadequate. We may thus ask the wrongdoer for the reasons why they acted, and if it becomes clear that they acted without excuse or justification, we may intend for them to come to see that they acted wrongly, and that this disposition issuing in the action is best resisted. This change would be produced by their recognition of forward-looking reasons to make it, such as their moral reform and reconciliation of impaired relationships. This makes the point of blaming (or protesting) clear to the one blamed, and we believe would be especially effective for building better beings. If the ground-level practice were instead entirely backward-looking, such forward-looking reasons would operate solely at the higher level of justification. This would represent a missed opportunity to make the point of blaming clear to wrong-doers. Vargas (2013), for instance, is open to forward-looking goals sometimes functioning in this way, despite his recommendation that the ground-level practice be largely backward-looking. In our view, practitioners generally being presented with the forward-looking reasons serves to enhance the practice overall.

Notice that there is a direct and transparent connection between reasons-responsiveness and this forward-looking notion of responsibility, while a similar tie is lacking for desert-invoking moral responsibility (Pereboom 2014a: 136–37). Responsiveness to reasons is clearly required for an agent to be subject to moral formation when blaming presents moral reasons to avoid the wrongdoing at issue and to act rightly instead. Because reconciliation also involves the wrongdoer accepting moral reasons to forbear from the behavior at issue, reasons-responsiveness is also required when reconciliation is the objective of such reasons-presenting blame. The link between reasons-responsiveness and an assumption of desert and the attended reactive attitudes is not similarly direct and transparent. Even if our desert-linked beliefs and reactive attitudes correlate with the perception that reasons-responsive agents have knowingly acted wrongly, the connection we see with the forward-looking reasons is absent.

In the remainder of this section, we expand on and consider some advantages of adopting this forward-looking, single-tier account of moral responsibility.

3.2 Blame and Anger

Many contend that blame is essentially an angry emotional response to wrongdoing, that someone is blameworthy just in case he's done wrong and merits an expression of anger for his wrongdoing. As David Shoemaker (2018) puts it, the blameworthy is the angerworthy. We raise three concerns about the choice of anger as the core emotional response in the account of blame. First, there are cases of blameworthiness that are plausibly not cases of angerworthiness (Pereboom 2021b: 41–42). Consider the following examples. Athena is a parent, and her teenage children misbehave in minor, common, predictable ways; they squabble, fail to clean their rooms, text their friends when they should be sleeping. Some parents would respond with anger, but Athena doesn't, and instead confronts them with protest for their behavior, guided by the duty to morally educate, but not with anger. The angry response is at best optional, in many such cases inappropriate. This is also the case for Basil, a high school teacher, whose students often misbehave in common ways. They come unprepared not having done the assigned reading, distract their classmates by talk not related to class material, and surf the internet instead of partici-pating and paying attention. Basil confronts them with moral protest, without anger. For both Athena and Basil, the angry response stands to be counter-productive and to undermine forward-looking effectiveness and respect, occasioning counterproductive reaction without moral improvement. Evidence for the inappropriateness of anger in these kinds of cases is that parents and teachers who express anger in such situations are routinely criticized for responding inappropriately.

A second concern, pointed out in Section 1, is that anger has a strong tendency to distort judgments of blameworthiness, and it's questionable whether being blameworthy is to be worthy of a reactive attitude that systemat-ically distorts precisely those judgments (Lerner, Goldberg, and Tetlock 1998; Goldberg, Lerner, and Tetlock 1999; Litvak et al. 2010; Pereboom 2021b: 42–43). A third concern for anger, also set out in Section 1, is that in disagree-ments closely tied to values, expressions of anger tend to occasion the backfire effect, an outcome in which value beliefs and related dispositions to act that are confronted with the aim of revision are strengthened and not weakened by the interaction (Nyhan and Reifler 2010, 2015; Harinck and van Kleef 2012).

3.3 Blame as Forward-Looking Moral Protest

In view of these problems for blameworthiness conceived as angerworthiness, one might instead endorse an account in which the stance of moral protest has pride of place (Hieronymi 2001; Talbert 2012; Smith 2013; Pereboom 2021b: 27–48). Here is a characterization:

> **Moral Protest Account of Blame:** For A to appropriately blame B is for A to adopt a stance of moral protest against B for immoral conduct that B has performed and that A is epistemically justified in attributing to B, and A's adopting this stance is morally justified. (Pereboom 2021b: 44)

The immoral conduct will typically be an immoral action or omission. At times blame is misplaced, because no wrong has been done, whereupon moral protest would count as blame but not as justified blame. For instance, Alex may adopt a stance of moral protest against Beth but believe falsely and without adequate justification that Beth acted wrongly, for example when Alex's belief is defectively motivated by anger or envy. It's possible that Callie believes truly and with epistemic justification that Damon acted wrongly and not be morally justified in adopting the stance of moral protest, if, for example, Damon is known by Callie to be mentally ill in a way that precludes the moral justifiability of blame.

Blame may have the objective, as on Hieronymi's (2001) proposal, of moral protest against someone for a past action that indicates an ongoing threat due to a persisting disposition to act in that wrongful way.

Moral protest may also be directed at the agent for having that disposition to act wrongly, without singling out a specific instance of wrongdoing. Still, not all appropriate moral protest need be focused on altering or eliminating dispositions to act wrongly. Blame as moral protest may, for example, have a role in a victim's recovery and restoration when the offender has already undergone reform.

3.4 A Moral Protest Account of Self-Blame

The stance of moral protest can also function in blaming oneself (Pereboom 2022: 48–52). One might see an action one has performed as wrong, and the disposition that issues in it as morally defective, and as a result take on a stance of opposition against oneself for having performed the action, a stance that includes opposition to one's acting wrongly in this general way based on moral reasons to refrain from it. In adopting this stance, one may aim at one's own moral formation or at reconciliation with someone one has wronged. If, for example, one has verbally abused a friend, and the relationship with him has been impaired as a result, one might assume a stance of protest against that past action with the aims of eliminating one's disposition to act wrongly in this way and of reconciliation with the friend.

In accord with Randolph Clarke's (2013) suggestion, in this context we might consider whether a wrongdoer deserves or basically deserves to feel guilt and the pain that it features (cf. Carlsson 2017; Duggan 2018). Clarke proposes, first, that there is value in the recognition by an agent who is blameworthy that he is blameworthy, and a further response, the feeling of guilt, provides a morally valuable and intuitively fitting addition to this acknowledgment. This response would have value insofar as it expresses moral concern for having done wrong and for those one has wronged.

To facilitate this discussion, let's adopt the convention – not intended to reflect ordinary language – for "guilt" to refer to an attitude that presupposes basic desert, in this case, one's basically deserving to feel pain accompanying the recognition that one has done wrong, and "regret" to refer to a similar attitude, which may typically involve feeling pain accompanying the recognition that one has done wrong, but without the presupposition that the pain is basically deserved. We contend that regret can be a morally fitting additional reaction to one's own wrongdoing, which can adequately play the moral role that guilt often has.

Two of our allies on this point, Bruce Waller (1990) and Hilary Bok (1998), argue that the fittingness of a pained feeling can be accounted for by coming to understand that one has done wrong without invoking desert at all. Bok provides an example in which one suffers a painful response upon recognizing one's wrongdoing, a response that she compares to heartbreak and thus does not involve a presupposition of desert (1998: 168–69). For a pertinent analogy, David Shoemaker provides a case in which a baseball player appropriately feels pain upon making a mistake while he doesn't deserve to feel this pain – our being fallible in sports is not up to us. Another kind of example is due to McKenna: it is appropriate to feel the pain of grief upon the death of a friend, while this pain is not deserved (see McKenna 2012, 2019). These cases feature the appropriateness of feeling pain without this being deserved. We contend that, similarly, it's appropriate for wrongdoers to feel regret for what they've done without the pain of regret being basically deserved, or deserved at all. But how might the feeling of pain upon recognition of wrongdoing be appropriate – and basically so – but not be basically deserved?

What's needed here is an indicator that distinguishes basically deserved pain from merely basically appropriate pain. One of us (Pereboom 2017c, 2021b: 50–51) along with Andreas Carlsson (2017) has suggested that the pain of guilt, due to its presupposition of desert, would be prima facie appropriately *imposed*, while the pain of grief would never be. We'll now try to make this suggestion more precise.

If pain were basically deserved upon wrongdoing, this would give rise to a moral permission for suitably situated agents to intentionally impose it on the wrongdoer for a non-instrumental reason. If a wrongdoer basically deserves to be punished, then there is a prima facie presumption that a parent (if the wrongdoer is her child) or state officials (if the wrongdoer is in the purview of their authority) are prima facie permitted to intentionally impose it on the wrongdoer for a non-instrumental reason. Guilt, given that it presupposes basic desert, would then involve pain appropriately intentionally imposed on oneself by oneself. The pain of grief lacks this feature. Despite grief and the pain that it involves being appropriate for someone who has experienced loss of a friend, no one is permitted to intentionally impose the pain of grief on her in such circumstances for a non-instrumental reason. One may inform the bereaved of the death of the friend, and it may be evident that she will feel the pain of grief as a result, but this does not amount to intentionally imposing the pain of grief for a non-instrumental reason. Thus the permissibility of imposition by suitably situated agents for a non-instrumental reason serves as a criterion for distinguishing basically deserved from non-basically deserved but appropriate pain.

Because in many cases of personal wrongdoing anger is not optimal or even appropriate, forgiveness should not generally be taken to involve renunciation of anger and its expressions. Setting aside skepticism about free will, in situations in which anger is appropriate, forgiveness may involve its renunciation. But in cases of wrongdoing in which the angry response is not appropriate, and one does not in fact respond with anger but rather with moral concern, one's forgiveness would not plausibly consist in the renunciation of anger and its expressions. This indicates that forgiveness may involve the renunciation of whatever blaming attitudes and their expressions are appropriate, where such attitudes differ across cases. This we accept, but even setting aside free will skepticism, we contend that forgiveness fairly generally involves the renunciation of the stance of moral protest (Pereboom 2021b: 103–22).

Imagine a friend has wronged you in some way a number of times by acting inconsiderately, and you find yourself resolved to end your friendship with him. You then challenge him in a moral conversation, protesting the wrong he has done and the threat to you that his disposition to behave in this way poses. In response, he is contrite, takes on a resolute disapproving stance toward that disposition, and commits himself to its elimination. You might now withdraw your protest and agree to continue with the relationship. On Hieronymi's proposal, forgiveness is such a withdrawal of moral protest to a threat upon acknowledgment of the offender's change of heart (Hieronymi 2001: 554).

Ratifying such a change of heart, we believe, generally involves renunciation of the appropriateness of the stance of moral protest against the wrongdoer for having committed the specific wrong that was the focus of the protest. This renunciation involves coming to believe that this stance is no longer appropriate in this case, together with a commitment not to engage in overt moral protest for the wrong at issue. This renunciation is compatible with the forgiver never having actually taken on the stance of moral protest, since in renouncing such a stance one may be renouncing the appropriateness of taking it on in the future.

4 Implications of Skepticism about Basic Desert

For many people, the main problem with the skeptical position about basic desert moral responsibility is not that there is considerable empirical evidence that it is false or that there is a challenging argument for its incoherence. The main concern is a practical one: Can we live with the belief that it is true? A number of skeptics argue that we, in fact, can (see, e.g., Pereboom 2001, 2014a, 2021b, 2022; Waller 2011, 2014; Caruso 2017, 2018a, 2021a, 2021b; Pereboom and Caruso 2018). In this section, we address three main classes of practical issues. The first concerns the extent to which the skeptic can retain our ordinary conception of morality. The second concerns the degree to which skepticism about basic desert moral responsibility coheres with the emotions required for the kinds of personal relationships we value. Lastly, we discuss the implications of the view for treatment of criminals.

4.1 Illusionism vs Optimistic Skepticism

Illusionism is the view that while we lack free will and moral responsibility, we should nonetheless promote *belief* in these notions since to disbelieve in basic desert moral responsibility would have dire consequences for society and ourselves (see Smilansky 1999, 2000, 2002, 2022). According to Saul Smilansky, one of the leading proponents of illusionism, most people not only believe in actual possibilities and the ability to transcend circumstances, but have "distinct and strong beliefs that libertarian free will is a condition for moral responsibility, which is in turn a condition for just reward and punishment" (2000: 26–27). Smilansky and other proponents of illusionism go on to argue that while our commonplace beliefs in free will and basic desert-entailing moral responsibility are illusions, if people were to accept this truth there would be wide-reaching negative intrapersonal and interpersonal consequences. It would be devastating, they warn, if we were to destroy such beliefs since the difficulties caused by "the absence of ultimate-level grounding" are likely to be great, generating "acute psychological discomfort" for many people and "threatening morality" (Smilansky 2000: 166). To avoid such deleterious social and personal consequences, and to prevent the unraveling of our moral fabric, illusionism contends that people should be allowed their positive illusion of free will and moral responsibility – i.e., we should not take these beliefs away from people, and for those of us who have already been disenchanted, we ought simply to keep the truth to ourselves.

In direct contrast to illusionism, is *disillusionism* (Nadelhoffer 2011): the view that to the extent that folk intuitions and beliefs about the nature of human cognition and moral responsibility are mistaken, philosophers and psychologists ought to do their part to educate the public – especially when their mistaken beliefs arguably fuel a number of unhealthy emotions and attitudes such as revenge, hatred, intolerance, or lack of empathy. Proponents of disillusionism typically point to the benefits of a world without the contested notion of moral responsibility. They cite the many instances in which practices that invoke it are counterproductive from a practical and humanitarian standpoint – notably in how they stifle personal development, encourage punitive excess in criminal justice, and perpetuate social and economic inequalities (see Waller 2011; Levy 2012; Caruso 2016, 2021b; Pereboom 2021a, 2021b, 2022). They maintain that if we abandon such moral responsibility "we can look more clearly at the causes and more deeply into the systems that shape individuals and their behavior" (Waller 2011: 287), and this will allow us to adopt more humane and effective interpersonal attitudes and approaches to education, criminal justice, and social policy.

A policy of disillusionism is also present in optimistic skepticism. Optimistic skeptics maintain that life without basic desert moral responsibility is not only possible, but preferable. Prospects of finding meaning in life or sustaining good personal relationships, for instance, would survive (Pereboom 2001, 2014a; Waller 2011; Caruso 2017, 2018a, 2021b). And although retributivism and severe punishment, such as the death penalty, would be ruled out, they argue that the imposition of sanctions could serve purposes other than the punishment of the guilty – e.g., it can also be justified by its role in incapacitating, rehabilitating, and deterring offenders (see Pereboom 2001, 2014a, 2021b; Vilhauer 2009a, 2013a and 2013b; Shaw 2011, 2019; Levy 2012, 2015; Corrado 2013, 2017; Caruso 2016, 2021b; Focquaert, Glenn, and Raine 2018; Pereboom and Caruso 2018; Focquaert 2019a).

4.2 Morality

The skeptical position requires rejection of our ordinary view of ourselves as blameworthy and praiseworthy in the basic desert sense. The concerns critics of this position have raised are often framed as targeting the rejection of moral responsibility in general. Peter van Inwagen, for example, writes:

> I have listened to philosophers who deny the existence of moral responsibility. I cannot take them seriously. I know a philosopher who has written a paper in which he denies the reality of moral responsibility. And yet this same philosopher, when certain of his books were stolen, said, "That was a *shoddy* thing to do!" But no one can consistently say that a certain act was a shoddy thing to do *and* say that its agent was not morally responsible when he performed it. (1983: 207)

Libertarian C.A. Campbell agrees and asserts that denying moral responsibility would destroy "the reality of the moral life" (1957). Defender of asymmetrical freedom Susan Wolf contends that if we deny moral responsibility, we must "stop thinking in terms of what ought not to be. We would have to stop thinking in terms that would allow the possibility that some lives and projects are better than others" (1981: 386). And compatibilist W.T. Stace flatly states, "it is certain that if there is no free will there can be no morality" (1952).

The contention that the sort of moral responsibility at issue in the debate, specifically, is a necessary condition for morality is directly challenged by a number of skeptics (see, Waller 1989, 2004, 2011, 2014; Pereboom 2001, 2014a, 2021b; Caruso 2021b; Caruso in Dennett and Caruso 2021). First, it appears false that all of morality would be undermined by the rejection of moral responsibility in any sense, whether or not it includes basic desert. In widely endorsed normative ethical views such as utilitarianism and Kantianism, moral judgments of right and wrong seem to be grounded independently of basic desert.

Utilitarians would reject the notion of basic desert if they contend, as they typically do, that all valid moral claims, including desert claims, are grounded in the principle that right actions are those that maximize expected utility. And several skeptics have argued that the core Kantian moral notions for grounding moral rightness and wrongness, the universalizability of moral maxims and the prohibition on treating persons merely as means, are independent of the notion of basic desert (Pereboom 2001: 150–52; Waller 2004: 429; Vilhauer 2013a, 2013b). If this is correct, Kantian accounts of moral rightness and wrongness can be endorsed while rejecting the contested basic desert sense of moral responsibility.

However, if determinism precludes basic desert blameworthiness, would it not also undercut judgments of moral obligation? Kant held that moral principles are for us principles of moral obligation, and he also famously argued that "ought" implies "can," that if the moral law commands that we *ought* to perform some action, it "inescapably follows" that we must be *capable* of performing that action (1781/1787/1987: A548/B576, 1785/1981: 94). G.E. Moore, following Kant, likewise argues that one "cannot say of anyone that he ought to do a certain thing, if it is a thing which it is physically impossible for him to do" (1922: 317). But if "ought" implies "can," and if because determinism is true agents could never have avoided acting as they do, it would be false that they ought to have acted otherwise (see Nelkin 2011: 100–1; cf. Jeppsson 2016). Furthermore, if an action is wrong for an agent just in case she is morally obligated not to perform it, determinism would then also undermine judgments of moral wrongness (Haji 1998).

There are, however, a number of ways a skeptic can respond to this criticism. One is to argue, as a number of philosophers do, that while the "ought" implies "can" principle (OIC for short) is widespread and deeply entrenched, it is nonetheless false (Sinnott-Armstrong 1984; Waller 2004, 2011; Graham 2011). Recent work in experimental philosophy suggests that the principle may not be as intuitive as philosophers think. Buckwalter and Turri (2015), Mizrahi (2015a), Chituc et al. (2016), and Henne et al. (2016) have all run experiments testing ordinary folk intuitions about the link between moral requirements and abilities. They independently found that commonsense morality rejects the OIC principle for moral requirements, and that judgments about moral obligations are made independently of considerations about ability. By contrast, they also found that judgments of *blame* were highly sensitive to considerations about ability, which suggests that commonsense morality might accept a "blame implies can" principle or that judgments of blame may play a modulatory role in judgments of obligation (see Buckwalter and Turri 2015; Chituc et al. 2016). These empirical findings lend support to Bruce Waller's claim that the OIC principle is a philosopher's invention infected by mistaken assumptions about moral responsibility (for further discussion, see Kurthy and Lawford-Smith 2015; Mizrahi 2015b; Kurthy, Lawford-Smith, and Sousa 2017; Cohen 2018).

Another option for skeptics is to accept OIC but adopt an *axiological* understanding of "ought" and an *epistemic* reading of this principle (Pereboom 2014a: 138–46). On this reading of the principle, when we say that an agent "ought to x," we can be understood as making an axiological (or value) judgment about x and accordingly recommending that the agent perform x at some future time. We can call this the *"ought" of axiological recommendation*. This is not the "ought" of moral obligation Kant and others may have had in mind, which in central cases issues a demand of an agent at some time to perform a specific action. Instead, when one tells an agent that she ought to refrain from performing an action of some type in the future, such action is being recommended on moral grounds. This use of "ought" should not be understood as presupposing a guarantee of a route actually accessible to an agent, via reasons for action, to acting in the recommended way. What is instead required is only that it is epistemically open that the agent act in the way recommended (for an objection, see Nelkin 2014; for a reply see Pereboom 2014b). Indeed, making such an "ought" judgment may well contribute to motivating the agent to act in the way recommended.

Yet another option for skeptics is to argue that while basically deserved blame and punishment is undermined by determinism, wrongdoing and obligation are not, for the reason that the notion of "can" required for moral obligation is less demanding than that needed for basic desert. David Brink argues that blame and obligation in this way differ in their sensitivity to possibility, and that in this respect morality mirrors criminal legal practice:

> But in the criminal law capacities and opportunities condition culpability or responsibility, not wrongdoing. Excuse is an affirmative defense that concedes wrongdoing but denies responsibility for wrongdoing. Insufficient capacity or opportunity is the basis for an excuse. So, in the case of a paradigmatic excuse, the lack of morally relevant alternatives precludes blame, not wrongdoing. The excused agent violates normative requirements and demands, but is not blameworthy for doing so. This means that blame is sensitive to possibility in a way that wrongdoing and obligation are not. This is a feature of the criminal law that sounds in morality as well. In both morality and criminal law we should reject voluntarism as a principle about obligation, duty, and requirement but accept it as a principle about the conditions under which blame is appropriate.
>
> (Brink 2021: 89; cf. Nelkin 2011: 110)

The skeptic about basic desert might agree with Brink that deserved blame is sensitive to possibility in a way that moral obligation is not – the standard of possibility for deserved blame is more demanding. The further claim (with which Brink, as a compatibilist, disagrees) is that this more demanding standard rules out (basically) deserved blame given causal determination, while moral obligation, together with wrongness, remain in place (Pereboom 2021b: 143–45).

Some critics, such as Shaun Nichols (2007), further object that if we stopped considering agents as blameworthy in the basic desert sense, we would be left with insufficient resources for addressing immoral behavior. In response, skeptics could turn to other senses of moral responsibility that have not been a focus of the free will debate. For instance, on the forward-looking, non-desert-based account of moral responsibility we favor (see Section 3), when we encounter immoral action, we might protest the behavior by asking the agent to consider what their actions indicate about their intentions and character, to demand apology, or to request reform, thereby having them consider reasons to behave differently in the future. From the skeptical perspective, then, much of our moral practices can vindicated by invoking any of several determinism-resistant accounts of moral obligation, and a forward-looking account of blame as moral protest.

One last concern we would like to address has to do with respect for persons. Some critics contend that if we give up belief in free will and basic desert moral responsibility, we would be unable to ground a special duty to respect persons or prohibit using them simply as a means-to-an-end (e.g., Smilansky 2005; Lemos 2013). John Lemos, for example, has argued that "the human capacity for moral responsibility gives human beings a special dignity and worth that is fundamental to a proper system of morality grounded on the concept of respect for persons" (2013: 78). This concern, however, seems misguided. There is no inconsistency in accepting a Kantian regard for respect for persons without accepting Kant's particular attitudes on free will (see Pereboom 2001: 150–52; Vilhauer 2009b, 2013a, 2013b; Caruso 2021a). Benjamin Vilhauer (2009b, 2013a, 2013b), for instance, has convincingly argued that there is an important, often overlooked, distinction between *action-based desert* claims and *personhood-based desert* claims. The former is the kind of desert claim at issue in the free will debate, while the latter is not. Consider the backward-looking justification of blame and praise, punishment and reward:

> [T]he only sort of reference event that mainstream ethicists typically accept in backward-looking justifications is action – more specifically, actions that they take agents to be morally responsible for performing (if they suppose that there are such things). According to backward-looking justifications of this form, we deserve to be treated in particular ways because of how we have acted. I . . . refer to such justifications as action-based desert claims. Since we can only deserve to be treated in particular ways based on our actions if we are morally responsible, action-based desert claims imply that the agent at issue acted with free will. (Vilhauer 2013b: 149)

Action-based desert claims therefore presuppose the control in action (i.e., free will) needed for basic desert moral responsibility.

Personhood-desert claims, on the other hand, arguably do not. This is because we can ground respect for persons in the Kantian principle that *persons must always be treated as ends, and never as mere means*, without adopting Kant's own particular views on free will. That is, instead of grounding respect for persons in a Kantian notion of transcendental (or libertarian) freedom, we can ground it in more naturalistic considerations. As Vilhauer explains, free will skeptics "can make such dignity and respect for persons a central moral principle if they respect people as rational agents rather than as free agents, and if they regard agents as autonomous not with respect of the laws of nature, but instead with respect to the undue influence of other agents" (2013b: 148). This is what Vilhauer means by personhood-desert claims:

> We need only look to the people with whom we are interacting to find a basis for desert-claims that constrain consequentialist justifications. Personhood can provide a basis for desert-claims which is irreducibly different from action, and which does not depend upon free will in the way action-based desert does. Persons deserve to be treated only as they would rationally consent to be treated, just because they are persons. (Vilhauer 2013b: 151)

Personhood-based desert claims are therefore distinct from action-based desert claims. And free will skeptics can recognize and appeal to the former, while rejecting the latter. Adopting the skeptical perspective is therefore also consistent with a duty to respect persons.

4.3 Personal Relationships

Is the assumption that we are morally responsible in the basic desert sense required for the sorts of personal relationships we value? The considerations raised by P.F. Strawson in his essay "Freedom and Resentment" (1962) suggest a positive answer. In his view, our justification for claims of blameworthiness and praiseworthiness is grounded in the system of human reactive attitudes, such as moral resentment, indignation, guilt, and gratitude. Strawson contends that because our moral responsibility practice is grounded in this way, the truth or falsity of causal determinism is not relevant to whether we justifiably hold each other and ourselves morally responsible. Moreover, if causal determinism were relevant and did threaten these attitudes, as the free will skeptic may maintain, we would face instead the prospect of the cold and calculating *objectivity of attitude*, a stance that relinquishes the reactive attitudes. In Strawson's view, adopting this stance would rule out the possibility of the meaningful sorts of personal relationships we value.

Strawson may be right to contend that adopting the objective attitude would seriously hinder our personal relationships (for a contrary perspective, see Sommers 2007). However, a case can be made that it would be wrong to claim that this stance would be appropriate if determinism did pose a genuine threat to the reactive attitudes (Pereboom 1995, 2001: 199–203, 2014a: 178–93, 2021b: 130–40; Pereboom and Caruso 2018; Caruso 2021a). As we saw in Section 2, given free will skepticism, an expression of resentment or indignation would involve doxastic irrationality when it is accompanied by the belief that the wrongdoer does not basically deserve the pain or harm of being its target. But relative to certain alternative emotional attitudes available to us, these reactive attitudes and their expressions may be suboptimal for interaction in relationships when wrongdoing is at issue. The alternative attitudes we have in mind are not threatened by free will skepticism because they are not connected with beliefs that conflict with this view, while at the same time they can effectively play the requisite roles in relationships (Pereboom 2001, 2014a; Nussbaum 2016).

Of the emotional attitudes associated with moral responsibility, resentment (directed toward an agent due to a wrong he has done to oneself) and indignation (directed toward an agent because of a wrong he has done to a third party) are especially closely connected with it. Expression of resentment and indignation has a communicative role in personal and societal relationships, and thus one might object that if we were to modify or eliminate these attitudes, communication in such relationships would be impeded. Against this, we hold that when we are wronged in our relationships there are other emotions available to us that are not challenged by skepticism about free will, whose expressions can also convey the relevant information. These emotions include feeling hurt or shocked or disappointed about what the offending agent has done, and sadness or sorrow and concern for them, and, most importantly, taking on the stance of moral protest against them for what they have done.

If moral protest, together with communication of sadness and sorrow, hurt and disappointment, is to take the place of expressions of resentment and indignation, the former attitudes would need to be fostered and promoted at the expense of the latter. It may well be that some types and certain degrees of resentment and indignation are beyond our power to alter, and hence even supposing that the free will skeptic is committed to doing what is right and rational, they might nevertheless be unable to eradicate these attitudes. But this supposition might be contested. Shaun Nichols (2007) cites the distinction between *narrow-profile* emotional responses, that is, immediate emotional reactions to situations, and *wide-profile* responses, which are not immediate and may involve rational control. Free will skeptics might expect that we will have limited success in altering narrow-profile, immediate resentment when we are seriously wronged in our intimate personal relationships. However, in wide-profile circumstances, we may have the ability to diminish, or even eliminate resentment, or at least disavow it in the sense of rejecting any force it might be thought to have in justifying painful or harmful reactions to the wrong done. This modification of moral anger might well be advantageous for our valuable personal relationships, and it stands to bring about the equanimity that Spinoza (1677/1985) thought free will skepticism, more generally, would secure.

Does valuable love, or else the best kind of love, require the freedom required for moral responsibility in the sense at issue in the free will debate, that is, the sense that involves basic desert? One might argue that valuable love must be deserved, and that the reasons for love incorporate free actions that deserve a loving response. Against this, parents typically love their newborn children without their having this sort of free will, and we think that such love is highly valuable (Pereboom 1995: 41, 2001: 202–24, 2014a: 190–93, 2018, 2021b: 123–40). Furthermore, when adults love each other, it is often due to factors that are not freely willed; appearance, intelligence, and affinities with persons or events in one's history may have a significant part. However, moral action and character are often especially important for occasioning and maintaining mature love that we value. But even if such love would be affected, such love would not be undercut if we came to believe that moral character and action do not come about through freely willed decision, for they would be loveable whether or not the beloved is thought to deserve praise for them. Valuable love involves wishing well for the other, taking on aims and projects of the other as one's own, cherishing the other for her own sake. Denying that the beloved has the free will required for desert does not undermine any of this.

Alternatively, one might argue that for love to be valuable, the loving response itself must be freely willed. Against this consideration, however, is the fact that parents' love for their children is often produced independently of the parents' will, and the same is true of romantic love, and these are kinds of love that we value highly (Pereboom 2001: 202–4, 2014a: 189–93, 2018). Robert Kane, for instance, agrees but contends that "there is a kind of love we desire from others – parents, children (when they are old enough), spouses, lovers and friends whose significance would be diminished … by the thought that they are determined to love us entirely by instinct or circumstances beyond their control or not entirely up to them" (Kane 1996: 88). The reason the significance of this love would then be diminished is that "to be loved by others in this desired sense requires that the ultimate source of others' love lies in their own wills" (Kane 1996: 88).

In response, we ask: in what sorts of cases does the will intuitively play a role in generating love for another at all? When an intimate relationship is faltering, people sometimes make a decision to try to make it succeed, and to attempt to regain the type of relationship they once had. When a student is housed in a dormitory with a roommate she didn't select, she might choose to make the relationship work. When a marriage is arranged by parents, the partners may decide to take steps to come to love each other. In such situations we might desire that someone make a decision to love, but it is not clear that we have reason to want the decision to be freely willed in the sense required for desert-involving moral responsibility. A decision to love on the part of another might significantly enhance one's personal life, but it is not obvious what value the decision's being free in this sense would add.

Moreover, while in these kinds of circumstances we might desire that someone else make a decision to love, we would typically prefer the situation in which the love was not mediated by decision. This is so not only for romantic attachments, but also for friendships and for relationships between parents and children.

One might propose that the will has a key role in maintaining love over an extended period. Søren Kierkegaard (1843/1971) suggests that a marital relationship ideally involves a commitment that is continuously renewed. Such a commitment involves a decision to devote oneself to the other, and thus, in his view, a marital relationship ideally involves a continuously repeated decision. A relationship with this sort of voluntary aspect might in fact be highly desirable. Nevertheless, it is difficult to see what might be added by these continuously repeated decisions being freely willed in the sense required for moral responsibility, by contrast with simply being a voluntary expression of what the agent deeply cares about. Thus although one might at first have the intuition that love that is freely willed is especially valuable, it is unclear exactly how such free will might have a desirable role in producing, maintaining, or enhancing love (Pereboom 2001: 202–4, 2014a: 190–93, 2018). We therefore propose that love, even in the sort featured in adult relationships or mutual regard, does not require the free will required for basic desert moral responsibility, or the conviction that we have it.

Lastly, gratitude arguably presupposes that the person to whom one is grateful is praiseworthy in the basic desert sense for a beneficial act (cf. Honderich 1988: 518–19). This may well be so. Still, certain aspects of gratitude would not be jeopardized by the skeptical view, and these aspects would seem to provide what is required for the personal relationships we value. Gratitude involves being thankful toward the person who has acted beneficially. This aspect of gratitude is in the clear – i.e., one can be thankful to a young child for some kindness without supposing that they are praiseworthy in the basic desert sense. Gratitude typically also involves joy as a response to what someone has done, and free will skepticism does not yield a challenge to being joyful and expressing joy when others act beneficially. Hence, the kind of gratitude we feel when we are thankful or joyful for some kindness is perfectly consistent with the rejection of basic desert moral responsibility.

4.4 Meaning in Life

Skepticism about basic desert moral responsibility also has the resources to respond to concerns that it undermines our sense of meaning in life (Pereboom 2001: 187–97, 2014a: 175–78, 2021b: 149–73). First, we may ask: would it be difficult for us to cope without a conception of ourselves as credit- or praise-worthy for achieving what makes our lives fulfilled, happy, satisfactory, or worthwhile – for achieving what Honderich calls our *life-hopes* (1988: 382ff.)? Life-hopes are aspirations for achievement, and it is natural to suppose that one cannot have an achievement for which one is not also praiseworthy in this sense, and thus giving up this kind of praiseworthiness would deprive us of our life-hopes. However, achievement and life-hopes are not as closely connected to basic desert praiseworthiness as this objection supposes. If someone hopes for a success in some project, and if they accomplish what they hoped for, intuitively this outcome would be an achievement of theirs even if they are not in this particular way praiseworthy for it. For example, if someone hopes that their efforts as a teacher will result in well-educated children, and they do, then there is a clear aspect in which they have achieved what they hoped for, even if because they are not in general morally responsible in the basic desert sense they are not praiseworthy in this way for their efforts.

One might, nevertheless, think that free will and basic desert skepticism would instill in us an attitude of resignation to whatever our behavioral dispositions together with environmental conditions hold in store. This, however, isn't clearly right. Even if what we know about our dispositions and environment gives us reason to believe that our futures will turn out in a particular way, it can often be reasonable to hope that they will turn out differently. For this to be so, it may be important that we lack complete knowledge of our dispositions and environmental conditions. Suppose that one reasonably believes that they have a disposition that might well be a hindrance to realizing a life-hope. But because they do not know whether this disposition will in fact have this effect, it remains open for them – that is, epistemically possible for them – that another disposition of theirs will allow them to transcend this obstacle. For instance, imagine that someone aspires to become a successful politician, but they are concerned that their fear of public speaking will get in the way. They do not know whether this fear will in fact frustrate their ambition, since it is open for them that they will overcome this problem, perhaps due to a disposition for resolute self-discipline to transcend obstacles of this sort. As a result, they might reasonably hope that they will conquer their fear and succeed in their ambition. Given skepticism about basic desert moral responsibility, if they in fact do overcome this difficulty and succeed in their political ambitions, this will not be an achievement of theirs in quite as robust a sense as we might naturally suppose, but it will be an achievement in a substantial sense nonetheless.

How significant is the aspect of our life-hopes that we must relinquish given the skeptical view? Smilansky argues that it would be quite significant, and as a result, "extremely damaging to our view of ourselves, to our sense of achievement, worth, and self-respect" (Smilansky 1997: 94), especially when it comes to achievement in the formation of one's own moral character. It's unclear, however, that this is correct. First, note that our sense of self-worth – our sense that we have value and that our lives are worth living – is to a non-trivial extent due to features not produced by our volitions, let alone free will. People place a great value on natural beauty, native athletic ability, and intelligence, none of which have their source in our volition. We also value voluntary efforts – in productive work and altruistic behavior, and in the formation of moral character. But even here, it doesn't much matter to us that these voluntary efforts are also freely willed in the sense at issue.

Consider how good character comes to be. It is plausibly formed to a significant degree by upbringing, and the belief that this is so is widespread. Parents regard themselves as having failed in raising their children if they turn out with immoral dispositions, and they typically take great care to bring their children up to prevent such an outcome. Accordingly, people often come to believe that they have the good moral character they do largely because they were raised with love and skill. But those that believe this about themselves seldom experience dismay because of it. We tend not to become dispirited upon coming to understand that good moral character is not our doing, and that we do not deserve a great deal of praise or credit for it. By contrast, we often feel fortunate and thankful. Suppose, however, that there are some who would be overcome with dismay. Would it be justified or even desirable for them to foster the illusion that they nevertheless deserve, in the basic sense, praise or credit for producing their moral character? We suspect that most would eventually be able to accept the truth without feeling much loss. All of this, we think, would also hold for those who come to believe that they do not deserve in the basic desert sense praise and respect for producing their moral character because they are not, in general, morally responsible in this way.

Our sense, then, is that even if we initially felt that free will and basic desert is essential to the fulfillment our successful projects confer on our lives, sufficient meaning can be secured by the sense of achievement that might be retained absent basic desert, by the appreciation for others engendered by recognizing the contribution they make to these accomplishments, and perhaps even, in accord with Spinoza's (1677/1985) conception, by a kind of gratitude occasioned by understanding that these successes are provided by a deterministic universe in which we have control only in a limited sense.

4.5 Basic Desert Skepticism and Criminal Behavior

Lastly, one of the most frequently voiced criticisms of skepticism about basic desert moral responsibility is that it is unable to adequately deal with criminal behavior and that the responses it would permit as justified are insufficient for acceptable social policy. This concern is fueled by two factors. The first is that one of the most prominent justifications for punishing criminals, *retributivism*, is incompatible with skepticism about basic desert. The second is that alternative justifications that are not ruled out by the skeptical view per se face significant independent moral objections (see Pereboom 2001, 2014a, 2021b; Boonin 2008; Zimmerman 2011; Caruso 2021b). Yet, despite this concern, we maintain that skepticism leaves intact other ways to respond to criminal behavior – in particular incapacitation, rehabilitation, and alteration of relevant social conditions – and that these methods are both morally justifiable and sufficient for good social policy. In this section, we present and defend our preferred model for dealing with dangerous criminals, an incapacitation account built on the right to self-protection analogous to the justification for quarantine (see Pereboom 2001, 2013, 2014a, 2021b; Caruso 2016, 2020, 2021b; Pereboom and Caruso 2018; Caruso and Pereboom 2020).

The retributive justification of legal punishment maintains that absent any excusing conditions, wrongdoers are morally responsible for their actions and *deserve* to be punished in proportion to their wrongdoing. Unlike theories of punishment that aim at deterrence, rehabilitation, or incapacitation, retributivism grounds punishment in the *blameworthiness* and *desert* of offenders. It holds that punishing wrongdoers is intrinsically good. For the retributivist, wrongdoers deserve a punitive response proportional to their wrongdoing, even if their punishment serves no further purpose. This means that the retributivist position is not reducible to consequentialist considerations nor in justifying punishment does it appeals to wider goods such as the safety of society or the moral improvement of those being punished. As a result, the *desert* invoked in retributivism is *basic* in the sense that it is not in turn grounded in forward-looking considerations.

The arguments for skepticism about basically deserved blame also count against retributivism. If agents do not deserve the harm and pain of blame just because they have knowingly done wrong, neither do they deserve the harm and pain of punishment just because they have knowingly done wrong. The challenge facing the basic desert skeptic, then, is to explain how we can adequately deal with criminal behavior without the justification provided by retributivism and basic desert. While some critics contend this cannot be done, skeptics point out that there are several alternative ways of justifying criminal punishment (and dealing with criminal behavior more generally) that do not appeal to the notion of basic desert and are thus not threatened by free will skepticism.

These include moral education theories, deterrence theories, and incapacitation theories justified by the right to harm in self-defense. While we maintain the first two approaches face independent moral mobjections – objections that, though perhaps not devastating, make them less desirable than their alternative – we argue that an incapacitation account built on the right to harm in self-defense provides the best option for justifying a policy for treatment of criminals consistent with free will skepticism.

Before turning to our positive account, let us say a few words about the first two alternative approaches.

Moral education theories draw an analogy with justification of the punishment of children. Children are typically not punished to exact retribution, but rather to educate them morally. Since moral education is a generally acceptable goal, a justification for criminal punishment based on this analogy is one the skeptic about basic desert moral responsibility can potentially accept. Despite its consistency with basic desert skepticism, a serious concern for this type of theory is that it is far from evident that punishing adult criminals is similarly likely to result in moral improvement. Children and adult criminals differ in significant respects. For example, adult criminals, unlike children, typically understand the moral code accepted in their society. Furthermore, children are generally more psychologically malleable than are adult criminals. Another concern is that it's unclear that punishment is even the best way to educate individuals morally. To return to the analogy of children, it was once thought acceptable to spank and/or slap children as a way to teach them about right and wrong. We no longer think such corporal punishment of children is ever acceptable. This is because we came to realize that corporal punishment does more harm than good and can cause long-term damage. The same may be true of criminal punishment generally. If so, then punishment would not have the desired morally educative benefits the theory presupposes. For these and other reasons, we see this approach as less desirable than an alternative incapacitation account (see Pereboom 2001: 161–66; Caruso 2021b: ch. 5).

Deterrence theories, especially utilitarian deterrence theories, have probably been the most discussed alternative to retributivism. According to deterrence theories, the prevention of criminal wrongdoing serves as the good on the basis of which punishment is justified. The classic deterrence theory is Jeremy Bentham's. In his conception, the state's policy on criminal behavior should aim at maximizing utility, and punishment is legitimately administered if and only if it does so. The pain or unhappiness produced by punishment results from the restriction on freedom that ensues from the threat of punishment, the anticipation of punishment by the person who has been sentenced, the pain of actual punishment, and the sympathetic pain felt by others such as the friends and family of the criminal (Bentham 1823/1948). On the other hand, the most significant pleasure or happiness that results from punishment derives from the security of those who benefit from its capacity to deter.

While deterrence theories are completely compatible with skepticism about basic desert moral responsibility, there are three general moral objections against them (e.g., Rawls 1955; McCloskey 1965; Smilansky 1990). The first is that they will justify punishments that are intuitively too severe. For example, it would seem that, in certain cases, harsh punishment would be a more effective deterrent than milder forms, while the harsh punishments are intuitively too severe to be fair. The second concern is that such accounts would seem to justify punishing the innocent. If, for instance, after a series of horrible crimes the actual perpetrator is not caught, it might maximize utility to frame and punish an innocent person. Such cases illustrate the "use" objection to utilitarianism, that it requires people to be harmed severely, without their consent, in order to benefit others, and this is often intuitively wrong.

Fortunately, there is an ethically defensible and practically workable alternative for dealing with dangerous crime that is not undercut by either free will skepticism or by other moral considerations. This theory is based on an analogy with quarantine and draws on a comparison between treatment of dangerous criminals and treatment of carriers of dangerous diseases. In its simplest form, it can be stated as follows: (1) Free will and basic desert skepticism maintains that criminals are not morally responsible for their actions in the basic desert sense; (2) plainly, many carriers of dangerous diseases are not responsible in this or in any other sense for having contracted these diseases; (3) yet, we generally agree that it is sometimes permissible to quarantine them, and the justification for doing so is the right to self-protection and the prevention of harm to others; (4) for similar reasons, even if a dangerous criminal is not morally responsible for his crimes in the basic desert sense (perhaps because no one is ever in this way morally responsible) it could be *as* legitimate to preventatively detain him as to quarantine the non-responsible carrier of a dangerous disease.

The first thing to note about the theory is that although one might justify quarantine (in the case of disease) and incapacitation (in the case of dangerous criminals) on purely utilitarian or consequentialist grounds, we resist this strategy. Instead, we maintain that incapacitation of the seriously dangerous is justified on the ground of the right to harm in self-defense and defense of others.

That we have this right has broad appeal, much broader than utilitarianism or consequentialism more generally has. In addition, this makes the view more resilient to a number of objections and provides a more resilient proposal for justifying criminal sanctions than other non-retributive options (see Pereboom 2001: 158–86, 2013, 2014a: 153–75, 2021b: 78–102; Caruso 2021b). One advantage it has, say, over consequentialist deterrence theories is that it has more restrictions placed on it with regard to using people merely as a means. For instance, as it is illegitimate to treat carriers of a disease more harmfully than is necessary to neutralize the danger they pose, treating those with violent criminal tendencies more harshly than is required to protect society will be illegitimate as well. In fact, the model requires that we adopt the *principle of least infringement*, which holds that the least restrictive measures should be taken to protect public health and safety. This ensures that criminal sanctions will be proportionate to the danger posed by an individual, and any sanctions that exceed this upper bound will be unjustified.

Second, the quarantine model places several constraints on the treatment of criminals. First, as less dangerous diseases justify only preventative measures less restrictive than quarantine, so less dangerous criminal tendencies justify only more moderate restraints. We do not, for instance, quarantine people for the common cold even though it has the potential to cause you some harm. Rather, we restrict the use of quarantine to a narrowly prescribed set of cases. Analogously, on this model the use of incapacitation should be limited to only those cases where offenders are a serious threat to public safety and no less restrictive measures were available. In fact, for certain minor crimes perhaps only some degree of monitoring could be defended. Second, the incapacitation account that results from this analogy demands a degree of concern for the rehabilitation and well-being of the criminal that would alter much of current practice. Just as fairness recommends that we seek to cure the diseased we quarantine, so fairness would counsel that we attempt to rehabilitate the criminals we detain. Rehabilitation and reintegration would therefore replace punishment as the focus of the criminal justice system. Lastly, if a criminal cannot be rehabilitated and our safety requires his indefinite confinement, this account provides no justification for making his life more miserable than would be required to guard against the danger he poses.

In addition to these restrictions on harsh and unnecessary treatment, the model also advocates for a broader approach to criminal behavior that moves beyond the narrow focus on sanctions. Most importantly, it situates the quarantine analogy within the broader justificatory framework of *public health ethics* (Caruso 2016, 2021b). Public health ethics not only justifies quarantining carriers of dangerous diseases on the grounds that it is necessary to protect public health, it also requires that we take active steps to *prevent* such outbreaks from occurring in the first place. Quarantine is only needed when the public health system fails in its primary function. Since no system is perfect, quarantine will likely be needed for the foreseeable future, but it should *not* be the primary means of dealing with public health.

The analogous claim holds for incapacitation. Taking a public health approach to criminal behavior would allow us to justify the incapacitation of dangerous criminals when needed, but it would also make prevention a *primary function* of the criminal justice system. So instead of focusing on punishment, the public health-quarantine model shifts the focus to identifying and addressing the systemic causes of crime, such as poverty, low socioeconomic status, systematic disadvantage, mental illness, homelessness, educational inequity, exposure to abuse and violence, poor environmental health, and addiction.

Since the *social determinants of health* and the *social determinants of criminal behavior* are broadly similar (see Caruso 2021b), the best way to secure public health and safety is to adopt a public health approach for identifying and taking action on these shared social determinants. Such an approach requires investigating how social inequities and systemic injustices affect health outcomes and criminal behavior, how poverty affects health and incarceration rates, how offenders often have pre-existing medical conditions including mental health issues, how homelessness and education affects health and safety outcomes, how environmental health is important to both public health and safety, how involvement in the criminal justice system itself can lead to or worsen health and cognitive problems, and how a public health approach can be successfully applied within the criminal justice system. We argue that just as it is important to identify and take action on the social determinants of health if we want to improve health outcomes, it is equally important to identify and address the social determinants of criminal behavior.

Furthermore, the public health framework sees *social justice* as a foundational cornerstone to public health and safety (Powers and Faden 2006; Caruso 2021b). In public health ethics, a failure on the part of public health institutions to ensure the social conditions necessary to achieve a sufficient level of health is considered a grave injustice. An important task of public health ethics, then, is to identify which inequalities in health are the most egregious and thus which should be given the highest priority in public health policy and practice. The public health approach to criminal behavior likewise maintains that a core moral function of the criminal justice system is to identify and remedy social and economic inequalities responsible for crime. Just as public health is negatively affected by poverty, racism, and systematic inequality, so too is public safety. This broader approach to criminal justice therefore places issues of social justice at the forefront. It sees racism, sexism, poverty, and systemic disadvantage as serious threats to public safety and it prioritizes the reduction of such inequalities.

By placing social justice at the foundation of the public health approach, the realms of criminal justice and social justice are brought closer together. We see this as a virtue of the theory since it is hard to see how we can adequately deal with criminal justice without simultaneously addressing issues of social justice. Retributivists tend to disagree since they approach criminal justice as an issue of individual responsibility and desert, not as an issue of prevention and public safety. It is a mistake, however, to think that the criteria of individual accountability can be settled apart from considerations of social justice and the social determinants of criminal behavior. Making social justice foundational, as our public health-quarantine model does, places on us a collective responsibility – which is forward-looking and perfectly consistent with skepticism about basic desert – to redress unjust inequalities and to advance collective aims and priorities such as public health and safety.

Summarizing the public health-quarantine model, then, the core idea is that the right to harm in self-defense and defense of others justifies incapacitating the criminally dangerous with the minimum harm required for adequate protection. The resulting account would not justify the sort of criminal punishment whose legitimacy is most dubious, such as death or confinement in the common kinds of prisons in the United States. The model also specifies attention to the well-being of criminals, which would change much of current policy. Furthermore, the public health component of the theory prioritizes prevention and social justice and aims at identifying and taking action on the social determinants of health and criminal behavior. This combined approach to dealing with criminal behavior, we maintain, is sufficient for dealing with dangerous criminals, leads to a more humane and effective social policy, and is actually preferable to the harsh and often excessive forms of punishment that typically come with retributivism.[3]

5 Final Words

In this Element, we discussed, in Section 1, a variety of different senses of responsibility and argued that the sense that has been of central philosophical and practical importance in contemporary debates is best understood in terms of the notion of basic desert. In Section 2 we examined the different skeptical arguments against our having basic desert moral responsibility, paying special

---

[3] For objections to the public health-quarantine model, see Smilansky (2011, 2017), Corrado (2016, 2018, 2019, 2021), Lemos (2016, 2018), Tadros (2017), Morse (2018), Kennedy (2021), Sifferd (2021), Walen (2021), Zaibert (2021), Donelson (forthcoming), and McCormick (forthcoming). For our replies to these objections, see Pereboom and Caruso (2018), Pereboom (2001, 2013, 2014a, 2016, 2020, 2021b), Caruso (2021b, 2021c, 2021d, forthcoming).

attention to the arguments for denying that we have the sort of control in action –
the free will – required for us to be morally responsible in this sense. In
Section 3 we set out an alternative forward-looking account of moral responsibility, which the skeptic about basic desert may endorse. It is grounded not in
basic or even non-basic desert, but in non-desert-invoking desiderata such as
protection, reconciliation, moral formation, and the recovery and restoration of
victims of wrongdoing. Such an account is arguably sufficient for addressing
moral and immoral behavior and for guiding our personal relationships. Finally,
in Section 4 we turned to concerns about the practical implications of the
skeptical view, such as whether it is consistent with morality more generally
and whether it can accommodate an adequate criminology, and to explaining
how the optimistic skeptic can respond to them.

References

Alicke, Mark D. (2000). "Culpable Control and the Psychology of Blame," *Psychology Bulletin* 126: 556–74.

Alicke, Mark D., David Rose, and Dori Bloom. (2012). "Causation, Norm Violation and Culpable Control," *Journal of Philosophy* 106: 587–612.

Bagley, Benjamin. (2017). "Properly Proleptic Blame," *Ethics* 127(4): 852–82.

Baker, Lynne R. (2006). "Moral Responsibility without Libertarianism," *Noûs* 40: 307–30.

Balaguer, Mark. (2010). *Free Will as an Open Scientific Problem*, Cambridge, MA: MIT Press.

Bennett, Christopher. (2002). "The Varieties of Retributive Experience," *Philosophical Quarterly* 52(207): 145–63.

Bentham, Jeremy. (1823/1948). *An Introduction to the Principles of Morals and Legislation*, New York: Macmillan.

Bohm, David. (1952). "A Suggested Interpretation of the Quantum Theory in Terms of 'Hidden' Variables, I and II," *Physics Review* 85(2): 166–93.

Bok, Hilary. (1998). *Freedom and Responsibility*, Princeton: Princeton University Press.

Boonin, David. (2008). *The Problem of Punishment*, Cambridge: Cambridge University Press.

Briggs, Jean. (1970). *Never in Anger: Portrait of an Eskimo Family*, Cambridge, MA: Harvard University Press.

Brink, David. (2021). *Fair Opportunity, Responsibility and Excuse*, Oxford: Oxford University Press.

Buckwalter, Wesley, and John Turri. (2015). "Inability and Obligation in Moral Judgment," *PloS One* 10(8): 1–20.

Campbell, Charles Arthur. (1957). *On Selfhood and Godhood*, London: George Allen & Unwin.

Capes, Justin. (forthcoming). "Manipulation and Direct Arguments," in *A Companion to Free Will*, Joseph Campbell, ed., New York: Wiley-Blackwell.

Carlsmith, Kevin M., and John M. Darley. (2008). "Psychological Aspects of Retributive Justice," *Advances in Experimental Social Psychology* 40: 193–236.

Carlsson, Andrea B. (2017). "Blameworthiness as Deserved Guilt," *The Journal of Ethics* 21: 89–115.

Caruso, Gregg D. (2012). *Free Will and Consciousness: A Determinist Account of the Illusion of Free Will*, Lanham: Lexington Books.

Caruso, Gregg D. (2016). "Free Will Skepticism and Criminal Behavior: A Public Health-Quarantine Model," *Southwest Philosophy Review* 32(1): 25–48.

Caruso, Gregg D. (2017). "Free Will Skepticism and the Question of Creativity: Creativity, Desert, and Self-Creation," *Ergo* 3(23): 591–607.

Caruso, Gregg D. (2018a). "Origination, Moral Responsibility, and Life-Hopes: Ted Honderich on Determinism and Freedom," in *Ted Honderich on Consciousness, Determinism, and Humanity*, Gregg D. Caruso, ed., pp. 195–216, London: Palgrave Macmillan.

Caruso, Gregg D. (2018b). "Skepticism About Moral Responsibility," in *The Stanford Encyclopedia of Philosophy*, Spring ed., Edward N. Zalta, ed. https://plato.stanford.edu/entries/skepticism-moral-responsibility/.

Caruso, Gregg D. (2019a). "A Defense of the Luck Pincer: Why Luck (Still) Undermines Moral Responsibility," *Journal of Information Ethics* 28(1): 51–72.

Caruso, Gregg D. (2019b). "Free Will Skepticism and Its Implications: An Argument for Optimism," in *Free Will Skepticism in Law and Society*, Elizabeth Shaw, Derk Pereboom, and Gregg D. Caruso, eds., pp. 43–72, New York: Cambridge University Press.

Caruso, Gregg D. (2020). "Justice without Retribution: An Epistemic Argument against Retributive Criminal Punishment," *Neuroethics* 13(1): 13–28.

Caruso, Gregg D. (2021a). "On the Compatibility of Rational Deliberation and Determinism: Why Deterministic Manipulation is Not a Counterexample," *Philosophical Quarterly* 71(3): 524–43.

Caruso, Gregg D. (2021b). *Rejecting Retributivism: Free Will, Punishment, and Criminal Justice*, Cambridge: Cambridge University Press.

Caruso, Gregg D. (2021c). "Rejecting Retributivism: Reply to Leo Zaibert," *The Philosopher* 109(4): 118–26.

Caruso, Gregg D. (2021d). "Retributivism, Free Will Skepticism, and the Public Health-Quarantine Model: Replies to Kennedy, Walen, Corrado, Sifferd, Pereboom, and Shaw," *Journal of Legal Philosophy* 46(2): 161–216.

Caruso, Gregg D. (forthcoming). "Preemptive Incapacitation, Victim's Rights, Desert, and Respect for Persons: Replies to McCormick and Donelson," *Journal of Practical Ethics*.

Caruso, Gregg D., and Stephen G. Morris. (2017). "Compatibilism and Retributivist Desert Moral Responsibility: On What is of Central Philosophical and Practical Importance," *Erkenntnis* 82(4): 837–55.

Caruso, Gregg D., and Derk Pereboom. (2020). "A Non-Punitive Alternative to Punishment," in *Routledge Handbook of the Philosophy and Science of Punishment*, Farah Focquaert, Bruce Waller, and Elizabeth Shaw, eds., pp. 355–65, New York: Routledge.

Chisholm, Roderick. (1964). "Human Freedom and the Self," The Lindley Lecture, Department of Philosophy, University of Kansas; reprinted in *Free Will*, Gary Watson, ed., pp. 24–35, Oxford: Oxford University Press, 1982.

Chisholm, R.M. (1976). *Person and Object: A Metaphysical Study*. La Salle: Open Court.

Chituc, Vladimir, Paul Henne, Walter Sinnott-Armstrong, and Felipe De Brigard. (2016). "Blame, Not Ability, Impacts Moral 'Ought' Judgments for Impossible Actions: Toward an Empirical Refutation of 'Ought' Implies 'Can'," *Cognition* 150: 20–25.

Clark, Cory J., James B. Luguri, Peter H. Ditto et al. (2014). "Free to Punish: A Motivated Account of Free Will Belief," *Journal of Personality and Social Psychology* 106(4): 501–13.

Clark, Cory J., Adam. Shniderman, James B. Luguri, Roy F. Baumeister, and Peter H. Ditto. (2018). "Are Morally Good Actions Ever Free?" *Consciousness and Cognition* 63: 161–82.

Clark, Cory J., Bo M. Winegard, and Roy F. Baumeister. (2019). "Forget the Folk: Moral Responsibility Preservation Motives and Other Conditions for Compatibilism," *Frontiers in Psychology* 10: Article 215, https://doi.org/10.3389/fpsyg.2019.00215, pp. 1–23.

Clarke, Randolph. (1993). "Toward a Credible Agent-Causal Account of Free Will," *Noûs* 27: 191–203.

Clarke, Randolph. (1996). "Agent Causation and Event Causation in the Production of Free Action," *Philosophical Topics* 24: 19–48.

Clarke, Randolph. (2003). *Libertarian Theories of Free Will*, New York: Oxford University Press.

Clarke, Randolph. (2005). "On an Argument for the Impossibility of Moral Responsibility," *Midwest Studies in Philosophy* 29: 13–24.

Clarke, Randolph. (2013). "Some Theses on Desert," *Philosophical Explorations* 16: 153–44.

Clarke, Randolph. (2019). "Free Will, Agent Causation, and 'Disappearing Agents'," *Noûs* 53(1): 76–96.

Cohen, Yishai. (2018). "An Analysis of Recent Empirical Data on 'Ought' Implies 'Can'," *Philosophia* 46(1): 57–67.

Corrado, Michael L. (2013). "Why Do We Resist Hard Incompatibilism? Some Thoughts on Freedom and Determinism," in *The Future of Punishment*, Thomas Nadelhoffer, ed., pp. 79–106, New York: Oxford University Press.

Corrado, Michael L. (2016). "Chapter Four: Quarantine and the Problem of the Third Man." UNC Legal Studies Research Paper No. 2849473. Available at SSRN: https://papers.ssrn.com/sol3/papers.cfm?abstract_id=2849473.

Corrado, Michael L. (2017). "Doing without Desert," in *Free Will and the Law: New Perspectives*, Allan McCay and Michael Sevel, eds., pp. 144–63, New York: Routledge.

Corrado, Michael L. (2018). "Criminal Quarantine and the Burden of Proof," *Philosophia* 47: 1095–110. https://link.springer.com/article/10.1007/s11406-018-0026-2.

Corrado, Michael L. (2019). "Fichte and the Psychopath: Criminal Justice Turned Upside Down," in *Free Will Skepticism in Law and Society: Challenging Retributive Justice*, Elizabeth Shaw, Derk Pereboom, and Gregg D. Caruso, eds., pp. 161–76, New York: Cambridge University Press.

Corrado, Michael L. (2021). "The Limits of the State's Power to Control Crime," *Journal of Legal Philosophy* 46(2): 126–31.

Cushman, FA. (2018). "Crime and Punishement: Differential Reliance on Causal and Intentional Information for Different Classes of Moral Judgment." *Cognition* 108: pp. 353–80.

d'Holbach, Paul-Henri Thiry. (1770). *Système de la Nature, ou Des Loix du Monde Physique et du Monde Moral*, Amsterdam: Marc-Michel Rey.

De Leersnyder, Jozefien, Michael Boiger, and Batja Mesquita. (2013). "Cultural Regulation of Emotion: Individual, Relational, and Structural Sources," *Frontiers in Psychology* 4: pp. 1–11.

Dennett, Daniel C. (1984). *Elbow Room*, Cambridge, MA: MIT Press.

Dennett, Daniel C. (2003). *Freedom Evolves*, New York: Viking Press.

Dennett, Daniel C., and Gregg D. Caruso. (2021). *Just Deserts*, Cambridge: Polity Press.

Donelson, Raff. (forthcoming). "Comments on Gregg Caruso's *Rejecting Retributivism*," *Journal of Practical Ethics*.

Doris, John. (2015). "Doing without (Arguing about) Desert," *Philosophical Studies* 172: 2625–34.

Duggan, Austin. (2018). "Moral Responsibility as Guiltworthiness," *Ethical Theory and Moral Practice* 21: 291–309.

Duggan, Austin. (2020). "A Genealogy of Retributive Intuitions," Unpublished.

Eccles, John. (1994). *How the Self Controls the Brain*, Berlin: Springer.

Ekstrom, Laura W. (2000). *Free Will: A Philosophical Study*, Boulder: Westview.

Ekstrom, Laura W. (2019). "Toward a Plausible Event-Causal Indeterminist Account of Free Will," *Synthèse* 196: 127–44.

Eshleman, Andrew. (2014). "Moral Responsibility," in *Stanford Encyclopedia of Philosophy*, Edward N. Zalta, ed. https://plato.stanford.edu/archives/win2016/entries/moral-responsibility/.

Everett, Jim A. C., Cory J. Clark, Peter Meindl et al. (2021). "Political Differences in Free Will Belief are Associated with Differences in Moralization," *Journal of Personality and Social Psychology* 120(2): 461–83.

Feinberg, Joel. (1970). "Justice and Personal Desert," in *Doing and Deserving*, pp. 55–94, Princeton: Princeton University Press.

Feldman, Gilad, Kin Fai Elick Wong, and Roy F. Baumeister. (2016). "Bad is Freer than Good: Positive-Negative Asymmetry in Attributions of Free Will," *Consciousness and Cognition* 42: 26–40.

Feltz, Adam. (2013). "Pereboom and Premises: Asking the Right Questions in the Experimental Philosophy of Free Will," *Consciousness and Cognition* 22(1): 53–63.

Fischer, John Martin. (1994). *The Metaphysics of Free Will*, Oxford: Blackwell.

Fischer, John Martin. (2004). "Responsibility and Manipulation," *The Journal of Ethics* 8: 145–77.

Fischer, John Martin. (2007). "Compatibilism" and "Response to Kane, Pereboom, and Vargas," in *Four Views on Free Will*, John Martin Fischer, Robert Kane, Derk Pereboom, and Manuel Vargas, eds., pp. 44–84, 184–90, Oxford: Blackwell.

Fischer, John Martin. (2014). "Review of *Free Will, Agency, and Meaning in Life*," *Science, Religion, and Culture* 1(3): 202–8.

Fischer, John Martin, and Mark Ravizza. (1998). *Responsibility and Control: A Theory of Moral Responsibility*, Cambridge: Cambridge University Press.

Flanagan, Owen. (2019). *The Geography of Morals: Varieties of Moral Possibility*, Oxford: Oxford University Press.

Flanagan, Owen. (2021). *How to Do Things with Emotions: The Morality of Anger and Shame Across Cultures*, Princeton: Princeton University Press.

Focquaert, Farah. (2019a). "Free Will Skepticism and Punishment: A Preliminary Ethical Analysis," in *Free Will Skepticism in Law and Society: Challenging Retributive Justice*, Elizabeth Shaw, Derk Pereboom, and Gregg D. Caruso, eds., pp. 207–36, New York: Cambridge University Press.

Focquaert, Farah. (2019b). "Neurobiology and Crime: A Neuro-Ethical Perspective," *Journal of Criminal Justice* 65. https://doi.org/10.1016/j.jcrimjus.2018.01.001.

Focquaert, Farah, Andrea L. Glenn, and Adrian Raine. (2018). "Free Will Skepticism, Freedom, and Criminal Behavior," in *Neuroexistentialism: Meaning, Morals, and Purpose in the Age of Neuroscience*, Gregg D. Caruso and Owen Flanagan, eds., pp. 235–50, New York: Oxford University Press.

Foster, John. (1991). *The Immaterial Self: A Defense of the Cartesian Dualist Conception of Mind*, New York: Routledge.

Frankfurt, Harry G. (1971). "Freedom of the Will and the Concept of a Person," *Journal of Philosophy* 68: 5–20.

Fricker, Miranda. (2016). "What's the Point of Blame? A Paradigm Based Explanation," *Nous* 50(1): 165–83.

Gert, Heather. (2018). "Awareness Luck," *Philosophia* 46: 131–40.

Ginet, Carl. (1997). "Freedom, Responsibility, and Agency," *The Journal of Ethics* 1: 85–98.

Goldberg, Julie H., Jennifer S. Lerner, and Philip E. Tetlock. (1999). "Rage and Reason: The Psychology of the Intuitive Prosecutor," *European Journal of Social Psychology* 29: 781–95.

Graham, Peter A. (2011). "'Ought' and Ability," *Philosophical Review* 120(3): 337–82.

Greene, Joshua, and Jonathan D. Cohen. (2004). "For the Law, Neuroscience Changes Nothing and Everything," *Philosophical Transactions of the Royal Society of London, Series B-Biological Sciences* 359: 1775–85.

Griffith, Meghan. (2010). "Why Agent-Caused Actions are Not Lucky," *American Philosophical Quarterly* 47: 43–56.

Haji, Ishtiyaque. (1998). *Moral Appraisability*, New York: Oxford University Press.

Harinck, Fieke, and Gerben A. Van Kleef. (2012). "Be Hard on the Interests and Soft on the Values: Conflict Issue Moderates the Effects of Anger in Negotiations," *British Journal of Social Psychology* 51: 741–52.

Harris, Sam. (2012). *Free Will*, New York: Free Press.

Hart, H. L. A. (1968). *Punishment and Responsibility*, New York: Oxford University Press.

Hasker, William. (1990). *The Emergent Self*, Ithaca: Cornell University Press.

Henne, Paul, Vladimir Chituc, Felipe De Brigard, and Walter Sinnott-Armstrong. (2016). "An Empirical Refutation of 'Ought' Implies 'Can'," *Analysis* 76(3): 283–90.

Hieronymi, Pamela. (2001). "Articulating an Uncompromising Forgiveness," *Philosophy and Phenomenological Research* 62: 529–55.

Honderich, Ted. (1988). *A Theory of Determinism*, Oxford: Oxford University Press.

Honderich, Ted. (2002). *How Free Are We?* New York: Oxford University Press.

Horst, Steven. (2011). *Laws, Mind, and Free Will*, Cambridge, MA: MIT Press.

Hume, David. (1739/1978). *A Treatise of Human Nature*, Oxford: Oxford University Press.

Hume, David. (1748/2000). *An Enquiry Concerning Human Understanding*, Oxford: Oxford University Press.

Jackson, Frank. (1998). *From Metaphysics to Ethics*, Oxford: Oxford University Press.

Jeppsson, Sofia. (2016). "Accountability, Answerability, and Freedom," *Social Theory and Practice* 42(4): 681–705.

Kane, Robert. (1996). *The Significance of Free Will*, New York: Oxford University Press.

Kant, Immanuel. (1781/1787/1987). *Critique of Pure Reason*, Paul Guyer and Allen Wood, trs., Cambridge: Cambridge University Press.

Kant, Immanuel. (1785/1981). *Grounding for the Metaphysics of Morals*, James Ellington, tr., Indianapolis: Hackett.

Kant, Immanuel. (1797/2017). *The Metaphysics of Morals*, Mary Gregor, tr., Cambridge: Cambridge University Press.

Kennedy, Chloe. (2021). "Taking Responsibility for Criminal Responsibility: Comments on *Rejecting Retributivism: Free Will, Punishment, and Criminal Justice*," *Journal of Legal Punishment* 46(2): 132–37.

Kierkegaard, Søren. (1843/1971). *Either/Or*, vol. 2, Walter Lowrie, tr., Princeton: Princeton University Press.

Kim, Jaegwon. (1999). "Making Sense of Emergence," *Philosophical Studies* 95: 3–36.

King, Matthew. (2013). "The Problem with Manipulation," *Ethics* 124(1): 65–83.

Kurthy, Miklos, and Holly Lawford-Smith. (2015). "A Brief Note of Ambiguity of 'Ought': Reply to Moti Mizrahi's 'Ought, Can, and Presuppositions: An Empirical Study'," *Methode* 4(6): 244–49.

Kurthy, Miklos, Holly Lawford-Smith, and Paulo Sousa. (2017). "Does Ought Imply Can?" *PloS One* 12(4): 1–24.

Leiter, Brain. (2007). "Nietzsche's Theory of the Will," *Philosophers' Imprint* 7: 1–15.

Lemos, John. (2013). *Freedom, Responsibility, and Determinism: A Philosophical Dialogue*, Indianapolis: Hackett.

Lemos, John. (2016). "Moral Concerns About Responsibility Denial and the Quarantine of Violent Criminals," *Law and Philosophy* 35: 461–83.

Lemos, John. (2018). *A Pragmatic Approach to Libertarian Free Will*, New York: Routledge.

Lenman, James. (2006). "Compatibilism and Contractualism: The Possibility of Moral Responsibility," *Ethics* 117: 7–31.

Lerner, Jennifer S., Julie H. Goldberg, and Philip E. Tetlock. (1998). "Sober Second Thought: The Effects of Accountability, Anger, and Authoritarianism on Attributions of Responsibility," *Personality and Social Psychology Bulletin* 24(6): 563–74.

Levy, Neil. (2009). "Luck and History-Sensitive Compatibilism," *Philosophical Quarterly* 59(235): 237–51.

Levy, Neil. (2011). *Hard Luck: How Luck Undermines Free Will and Moral Responsibility*, Oxford: Oxford University Press.

Levy, Neil. (2012). "Skepticism and Sanction: *The Benefits of Rejecting Moral Responsibility*," *Law and Philosophy* 31: 477–93.

Levy, Neil. (2015). "Less Blame, Less Crime? The Practical Implications of Moral Responsibility Skepticism," *Journal of Practical Ethics* 3(2): 1–17.

Lewis, Peter J. (2016). *Quantum Ontology: A Guide to the Metaphysics of Quantum Mechanics*, New York: Oxford University Press.

Litvak, Paul M., Jennifer S. Lerner, Larissa Z. Tiedens, and Katherine Shonk. (2010). "Fuel in the Fire: How Anger Impacts Judgments and Decision Making," in *International Handbook of Anger*, Michael Potegal, Gerhard Stemmler, and Charles Spielberger, eds., pp. 287–301, New York: Springer.

Lucretius. (50 BCE/1998). *On the Nature of the Universe*, Ronald Melville, tr., Oxford: Oxford University Press.

Lycan, William G. (1987). *Consciousness*, Cambridge, MA: MIT Press.

McCloskey, Henry J. (1965). "A Non-Utilitarian Approach to Punishment," *Inquiry* 8: 249–63.

McCormick, Kelly. (forthcoming). "Comments on Gregg Caruso's *Rejecting Retributivism: Free Will, Punishment, and Criminal Justice*," *Journal of Practical Ethics*.

McGeer, Victoria. (2015). "Building a Better Theory of Responsibility," *Philosophical Studies* 172(10): 2635–49.

McKenna, Michael. (2008). "A Hard-Line Reply to Pereboom's Four-Case Manipulation Argument," *Philosophy and Phenomenological Research* 77: 142–59.

McKenna, Michael. (2012). *Conversation and Responsibility*, New York: Oxford University Press.

McKenna, Michael. (2014). "Revisiting the Manipulation Argument: A Hard-Liner Takes It on the Chin," *Philosophy and Phenomenological Research* 87(2): 467–87.

McKenna, Michael. (2019). "Basically Deserved Blame and its Value," *Journal of Ethics and Social Philosophy* 15: 255–82.

McKenna, Michael, and Derk Pereboom. (2016). *Free Will: A Contemporary Introduction*, New York: Routledge.

Mele, Alfred. (2006). *Free Will and Luck*, New York: Oxford University Press.

Mele, Alfred. (2008). "Manipulation, Compatibilism, and Moral Responsibility," *The Journal of Ethics* 12: 263–86.

Milam, Per-Erik. (2016). "Reactive Attitudes and Personal Relationships," *Canadian Journal of Philosophy* 42: 102–22.

Mizrahi, Moti. (2015a). "Ought, Can, and Presupposition: An Experimental Study," *Methode* 4(6): 232–43.

Mizrahi, Moti. (2015b). "Ought, Can, and Presupposition: A Reply to Kurthy and Lawford-Smith," *Methode* 4(6): 250–56.

Moore, G. E. (1922). *Ethics*, Oxford: Oxford University Press.

Morris, Stephen. (2009). "The Impact of Neuroscience on the Free Will Debate," *Florida Philosophical Review* 9(2): 56–78.

Morris, Stephen. (2015). *Science and the End of Ethics*, New York: Palgrave Macmillan.

Morris, Stephen. (2018). "The Implications of Rejecting Free Will: An Empirical Analysis." *Philosophical Psychology* 31(2): 299–321.

Morse, Stephen J. (2004). "Reasons, Results, and Criminal Responsibility," *University of Illinois Law Review* 2004: 363–444.

Morse, Stephen J. (2016). "The Inevitable Mind in the Age of Neuroscience," in *Philosophical Foundations of Law and Neuroscience*, Dennis Patterson and Michael S. Pardo, eds., pp. 29–50, New York: Oxford University Press.

Morse, Stephen J. (2018). "The Neuroscientific Non-Challenge to Meaning, Morals, and Purpose," in *Neuroexistentialism: Meaning, Morals, and Purpose in the Age of Neuroscience*, Gregg D. Caruso and Owen Flanagan, eds., pp. 333–58, New York: Oxford University Press.

Murphy, Jeffrie G. (1988). "Hatred: A Qualified Defense," in *Forgiveness and Mercy*, Jeffrie G. Murphy and Jean Hampton, eds., pp. 88–110, Cambridge: Cambridge University Press.

Murray, Dylan, and Tania Lombrozo. (2017). "Effects of Manipulation on Attributions of Causation, Free Will, and Moral Responsibility," *Cognitive Science* 41: 447–81.

Nadelhoffer, Thomas. (2006). "Bad Acts, Blameworthy Agents, and Intentional Action: Some Problems for Jury Impartiality," *Philosophical Explorations* 9: 203–20.

Nadelhoffer, Thomas. (2011). "The Threat of Shrinking Agency and Free Will Disillusionism," in *Conscious Will and Responsibility*, Lynne Nadel and Walter Sinnott-Armstrong, eds., pp. 173–88, Oxford: Oxford University Press.

Nahmias, Eddy. (2014). "Is Free Will an Illusion? Confronting Challenges from the Modern Mind Sciences," in *Moral Psychology*, vol. 4, Walter Sinnott-Armstrong, ed., pp. 1–25, Cambridge, MA: MIT Press.

Nelkin, Dana K. (2004/2013). "Moral Luck," in *Stanford Encyclopedia of Philosophy* Edward N. Zalta, ed., https://plato.stanford.edu/entries/moral-luck/.

Nelkin, Dana K. (2011). *Making Sense of Freedom and Responsibility*, Oxford: Oxford University Press.

Nelkin, Dana K. (2014). "Free Will Skepticism and Obligation Skepticism: Comments on Derk Pereboom's *Free Will, Agency, and Meaning in Life*," *Science, Religion and Culture* 1(3): 209–17.

Nichols, Shaun. (2007). "After Compatibilism: A Naturalistic Defense of the Reactive Attitudes," *Philosophical Perspectives* 21: 405–28.Nichols, Shaun. (2015). *Bound*, Oxford: Oxford University Press.

Nietzsche, Friedrich. (1888/1954). *Twilight of the Idols*, Walter Kaufmann, tr., New York: Viking.

Nussbaum, Martha. (2016). *Anger and Forgiveness*, Oxford: Oxford University Press.

Nyhan, Brendan, and Jason Reifler. (2010). "When Corrections Fail: The Persistence of Political Misperceptions," *Political Behavior* 32: 303–30.

Nyhan, Brendan, and Jason Reifler. (2015). "Does Correcting Myths about the Flu Vaccine Work? An Experimental Evaluation of the Effects of Corrective Information," *Vaccine* 33: 459–64.

O'Connor, Timothy. (2000). *Persons and Causes*, New York: Oxford University Press.

O'Connor, Timothy. (2008). "Agent-Causal Power," in *Dispositions and Causes*, Toby Handfield, ed., pp. 189–214, Oxford: Oxford University Press.

Papineau, David. (2002). *Thinking About Consciousness*, New York: Oxford University Press.

Pereboom, Derk. (1995). "Determinism Al Dente," *Noûs* 29: 21–45.

Pereboom, Derk. (2001). *Living without Free Will*, Cambridge: Cambridge University Press.

Pereboom, Derk. (2008). "A Hard-Line Reply to the Multiple-Case Manipulation Argument," *Philosophy and Phenomenological Research* 77: 160–70.

Pereboom, Derk. (2013). "Free Will Skepticism and Criminal Responsibility," in *The Future of Punishment*, Thomas Nadelhoffer, ed., pp. 49–78, New York: Oxford University Press.

Pereboom, Derk. (2014a). *Free Will, Agency, and Meaning in Life*, Oxford: Oxford University Press.

Pereboom, Derk. (2014b). "Responses to John Fischer and Dana Nelkin," *Science, Religion, and Culture* 1(3): 218–25.

Pereboom, Derk. (2016). "A Defense of Free Will Skepticism: Replies to Commentaries by Victor Tadros, Saul Smilansky, Michael McKenna, and

Alfred R. Mele on *Free Will, Agency, and Meaning in Life*," *Criminal Law and Philosophy* 11(3): 1–20.

Pereboom, Derk. (2017a). "Response to Daniel Dennett on Free Will Skepticism," *Rivista Internazionale di Filosofia e Psicologia* 8: 259–65.

Pereboom, Derk. (2017b). "Responsibility, Agency, and the Disappearing Agent Objection," in *Le Libre- Arbitre, approches contemporaines*, Jean-Baptiste Guillon, ed., pp. 1–18, Paris: Collège de France.

Pereboom, Derk. (2017c). "Responsibility, Regret, and Protest," in *Oxford Studies in Agency and Responsibility*, vol. 4, David Shoemaker, ed., pp. 121–40, Oxford: Oxford University Press.

Pereboom, Derk. (2018). "Love and Freedom," in *The Oxford Handbook of the Philosophy of Love*, Christopher Grau and Aaron Smuts, eds., pp. 123–76, New York: Oxford University Press.

Pereboom, Derk. (2020). "Incapacitation, Reintegration, and Limited General Deterrence," *Neuroethics* 13: 87–97.

Pereboom, Derk. (2021a). "Undivided Forward-Looking Moral Responsibility," *The Monist* 104(4): 484–97.

Pereboom, Derk. (2021b). *Wrongdoing and the Moral Emotions*, Oxford: Oxford University Press.

Pereboom, Derk. (2022). *Free Will*, Cambridge Elements in Philosophy, Cambridge: Cambridge University Press.

Pereboom, Derk, and Gregg D. Caruso. (2018). "Hard-Incompatibilist Existentialism: Neuroscience, Punishment, and Meaning in Life," in *Neuroexistentialism: Meaning, Morals, and Purpose in the Age of Neuroscience*, Gregg D. Caruso and Owen Flanagan, eds., pp. 193–222, New York: Oxford University Press.

Pickard, Hannah. (2013). "Irrational Blame," *Analysis* 73(4): 613–26.

Powers, Madison, and Ruth Faden. (2006). *Social Justice: The Moral Foundations of Public Health Policy*, New York: Oxford University Press.

Priestley, Joseph. (1778/1965). "A Free Discussion of the Doctrines of Materialism and Philosophical Necessity," in *A Correspondence between Dr. Price and Dr. Priestley, London: Joseph Johnson*, 1778, Part III; reprinted in Joseph Priestley, *Priestley's Writings on Philosophy, Science, and Politics*, John Passmore, ed., New York: Collier.

Rawls, John. (1955). "Two Concepts of Rules," *Philosophical Review* 64: 3–32.

Reid, Thomas. (1788/1983). *Essays on the Active Powers of Man*, in *The Works of Thomas Reid, D.D.*, Sir William Hamilton, ed., Hildesheim: G. Olms Verlagsbuchhandlung.

Richards, Janet Radcliffe. (2000). *Human Nature after Darwin: A Philosophical Introduction*, New York: Routledge.

Rosen, Gideon. (2004). "Skepticism about Moral Responsibility," *Philosophical Perspectives* 18: 295–313.

Rudy-Hiller, Fernando. (2018). "The Epistemic Condition for Moral Responsibility," in *Stanford Encyclopedia of Philosophy*, Edward N. Zalta and Uri Nodelman eds., https://plato.stanford.edu/entries/moral-responsibility-epistemic/.

Śāntideva. (700/1995). *The Bodhicaryāvaātra*, Kate Crosby and Andrew Skilton, trs., New York: Oxford University Press.

Sapolsky, Robert M. (2017). *Behave: The Biology of Humans at Our Best and Worst*, London: Penguin.

Sartorio, Carolina. (2016). *Causation and Free Will*, Oxford: Oxford University Press.

Scanlon, Thomas M. (1998). *What We Owe to Each Other*, Boston: Harvard University Press.

Scanlon, Thomas M. (2013). "Giving Desert Its Due," *Philosophical Explorations* 16: 101–16.

Schopenhauer, Arthur. (1818/1961). *The World as Will and Idea* (later translated as *The World as Will and Representation*), Richard Burdon Haldane and John Kemp, trs., Garden City: Doubleday.

Shabo, Seth. (2012). "Where Love and Resentment Meet: Strawson's Interpersonal Defense of Compatibilism," *Philosophical Review* 121: 95–124.

Shariff, Azim F., Joshua D. Greene, Johan C. Karremans et al. (2014). "Free Will and Punishment: A Mechanistic View of Human Nature Reduces Retribution," *Psychological Science* 25(8): 1563–70.

Shaw, Elizabeth. (2011). "Free Will, Punishment and Neurotechnologies," in *Technologies on the Stand: Legal and Ethical Questions in Neuroscience and Robotics*, Bibi van den Berg and Laura Klaming, eds., pp. 177–94, Nijmegen: Wolf Legal.

Shaw, Elizabeth. (2019). "Justice without Moral Responsibility?" *Journal of Information Ethics* 28(1): 95–114.

Shoemaker, David. (2011). "Attributability, Answerability, and Accountability: Toward a Wider Theory of Moral Responsibility," *Ethics* 121: 602–32.

Shoemaker, David. (2015). *Responsibility from the Margins*, Oxford: Oxford University Press.

Shoemaker, David. (2018). "You Oughta Know: Defending Angry Blame," in *The Moral Psychology of Anger*, Mysha Cherry and Owen Flanagan, eds., pp. 67–88, Lanham, MD: Rowman & Littlefield.

Sifferd, Katrina. (2006). "In Defense of the Use of Commonsense Psychology in the Criminal Law," *Law and Philosophy* 25(6): 571–612.

Sifferd, Katrina. (2014). "What Does It Mean to Be a Mechanism? Stephen Morse, Non-Reductivism, and Mental Causation," *Criminal Law and Philosophy* 11: 143–59.

Sifferd, Katrina. (2021). "Why Not 'Weak' Retributivism?" *Journal of Legal Philosophy* 46(2): 138–43.

Sinnott-Armstrong, Walter. (1984). "'Ought' Conversationally Implies 'Can'," *Philosophical Review* 93(2): 249–61.

Slattery, 'Trick. (2014). *Breaking the Free Will Illusion for the Betterment of Humankind*, Working Matter Publishing.

Slote, Michael. (1990). "Ethics without Free Will," *Social Theory and Practice* 16: 369–83.

Smilansky, Saul. (1990). "Utilitarianism and the 'Punishment' of the Innocent: The General Problem," *Analysis* 50: 256–61.

Smilansky, Saul. (1997). "Can a Determinist Help Herself?" in *Freedom and Responsibility: General and Jewish Perspectives*, Charles H. Manekin and Menachem M. Kellner, eds., pp. 85–98, College Park: University of Maryland Press.

Smilansky, Saul. (1999). "Free Will: The Positive Role of Illusion," *The Proceedings of the Twentieth World Congress of Philosophy*, Bowling Green: Philosophy Document Center 2: 143–52.

Smilansky, Saul. (2000). *Free Will and Illusion*, New York: Oxford University Press.

Smilansky, Saul. (2002). "Free Will, Fundamental Dualism, and the Centrality of Illusion," in *The Oxford Handbook of Free Will*, Robert Kane, ed., pp. 249–505, New York: Oxford University Press.

Smilansky, Saul. (2005). "Free Will and Respect for Persons," *Midwest Studies in Philosophy* 29: 248–61.

Smilansky, Saul. (2011). "Hard Determinism and Punishment: A Practical Reductio," *Law and Philosophy* 30: 353–67.

Smilansky, Saul. (2012). "Review of Bruce N. Waller's *Against Moral Responsibility*," *Notre Dame Philosophical Review*. https://ndpr.nd.edu/reviews/against-moral-responsibility/.

Smilansky, Saul. (2017). "Pereboom on Punishment: Funishment, Innocence, Motivation, and Other Difficulties," *Criminal Law and Philosophy* 11: 591–603.

Smilansky, Saul. (2022). "Illusionism," in *The Oxford Handbook on Moral Responsibility*, Dana Kay Nelkin and Derk Pereboom, eds., pp. 203–21, New York: Oxford University Press.

Smith, Angela. (2012). "Attributability, Answerability, and Accountability: In Defense of a Unified Account," *Ethics* 122(3): 575–89.

Smith, Angela. (2013). "Moral Blame and Moral Protest," in *Blame: Its Nature and Norms*, D. Justin Coates and Neal A. Tognazzini, eds., pp. 27–48, New York: Oxford University Press.

Sommers, Tamler. (2007). "The Objective Attitude," *Philosophical Quarterly* 57: 321–41.

Sommers, Tamler. (2012). *Relative Justice: Cultural Diversity, Free Will, and Moral Responsibility*, Princeton: Princeton University Press.

Spinoza, Benedictus. (1677/1985). *Ethics*, in *The Collected Works of Spinoza*, vol. 1, Edwin Curley, ed. and tr., pp. 408–620, Princeton: Princeton University Press.

Stace, Walter T. (1952). *Religion and the Modern Mind*, New York: Lippincott.

Steward, Helen. (2012). *A Metaphysics for Freedom*, New York: Oxford University Press.

Strawson, Galen. (1986). *Freedom and Belief*, Oxford: Oxford University Press.

Strawson, Galen. (1994). "The Impossibility of Moral Responsibility," *Philosophical Studies* 75: 5–24.

Strawson, Peter F. (1962). "Freedom and Resentment," *Proceedings of the British Academy* 48: 187–211.

Swinburne, Richard. (1996). *The Evolution of the Soul*, Oxford: Clarendon Press.

Tadros, Victor. (2017). "Doing without Desert," *Criminal Law and Philosophy* 11: 605–16.

Talbert, Matthew. (2012). "Moral Competence, Moral Blame, and Protest," *Journal of Ethics* 16: 89–101.

Talbert, Matthew. (2016). *Moral Responsibility: An Introduction*, Cambridge: Polity.

Taylor, Richard. (1966). *Action and Purpose*, Englewood Cliffs: Prentice-Hall.

Taylor, Richard. (1974). *Metaphysics*, 4th ed., Englewood Cliffs: Prentice-Hall.

Telech, Daniel. (2021). "Praise as Moral Address," in *Oxford Studies in Agency and Responsibility*, vol. 7, David Shoemaker, ed., pp. 154–81, Oxford: Oxford University Press.

Tognazzini, Neal A. (2014). "The Structure of a Manipulation Argument," *Ethics* 124(2): 358–69.

Trevors, Gregory J., Krista R. Muis, Reinhard Pekrun, Gale M. Sinatra, and Philip H. Winne. (2016). "Identity and Epistemic Emotions During Knowledge Revision: A Potential Account for the Backfire Effect," *Discourse Processes* 53(5–6): 339–70.

Vaidman, Lev. (2014). "Quantum Theory and Determinism," *Quantum Studies: Mathematics and Foundations* 1: 5–38.

van Inwagen, Peter. (1983). *An Essay on Free Will*, Oxford: Oxford University Press.

Vargas, Manuel. (2007). "Revisionism" and "Response to Fischer, Kane, and Pereboom," in *Four Views on Free Will*, John Martin Fischer, Robert Kane, Derk Pereboom, and Manuel Vargas, eds., pp. 126–65, 204–19, Oxford: Blackwell.

Vargas, Manuel. (2013). *Building Better Beings*, New York: Oxford University Press.

Vargas, Manuel. (2015). "Desert, Responsibility, and Justification: A Reply to Doris, McGeer, and Robinson," *Philosophical Studies* 172: 2659–78.

Vilhauer, Benjamin. (2004). "Hard Determinism, Remorse, and Virtue Ethics," *Southern Journal of Philosophy* 42: 547–64.

Vilhauer, Benjamin. (2009a). "Free Will and Reasonable Doubt," *American Philosophical Quarterly* 46: 131–40.

Vilhauer, Benjamin. (2009b). "Free Will Skepticism and Personhood as a Desert Base," *Canadian Journal of Philosophy* 39: 489–511.

Vilhauer, Benjamin. (2012). "Taking Free Will Skepticism Seriously," *Philosophical Quarterly* 62: 833–52.

Vilhauer, Benjamin. (2013a). "The People Problem," in *Exploring the Illusion of Free Will and Moral Responsibility*, Gregg D. Caruso, ed., pp. 141–60, Lanham, MD: Lexington Books.

Vilhauer, Benjamin. (2013b). "Persons, Punishment, and Free Will Skepticism," *Philosophical Studies* 162: 143–63.

Walen, Alec. (2021). "Determinism, Compatibilism, and Basic Desert: A Reply to Gregg Caruso," *Journal of Legal Philosophy* 46(2): 144–48.

Wallace, R. Jay. (1994). *Responsibility and the Moral Sentiments*, Cambridge, MA: Harvard University Press.

Waller, Bruce. (1989). "Denying Responsibility: The Difference it Makes," *Analysis* 49(1): 44–47.

Waller, Bruce. (1990). *Freedom without Responsibility*, Philadelphia: Temple University Press.

Waller, Bruce. (2004). "Virtue Unrewarded: Morality without Moral Responsibility," *Philosophia* 31(3–4): 427–47.

Waller, Bruce. (2011). *Against Moral Responsibility*, Cambridge, MA: MIT Press.

Waller, Bruce. (2014). *The Stubborn System of Moral Responsibility*, Cambridge, MA: MIT Press.

Watson, Gary. (1987). "Responsibility and the Limits of Evil," in *Responsibility, Character, and the Emotions*, Ferdinand Schoeman, ed., pp. 256–86, Cambridge: Cambridge University Press.

Watson, Gary. (1996). "Two Faces of Responsibility," *Philosophical Topics* 24: 227–48.

Wegner, Daniel. (2002). *The Illusion of Conscious Will*, Cambridge, MA: MIT Press.

Wolf, Susan. (1981). "The Importance of Free Will," *Mind* 90(359): 386–405.

Wolf, Susan. (2011). "Blame, Italian Style," in *Reasons and Cognition: Essays on the Philosophy of T.M. Scanlon*, R. Jay Wallace, Rahul Kumar, and Samuel Freeman, eds., pp. 332–47 New York: Oxford University Press.

Zaibert, Leo. (2021). "Embracing Retributivism," *The Philosopher* 109(4): 105–17.

Zimmerman, Michael. (2011). *The Immorality of Punishment*, Petersborough: Broadview Press.

Cambridge Elements

Ethics

Ben Eggleston

University of Kansas

Ben Eggleston is a professor of philosophy at the University of Kansas. He is the editor of
John Stuart Mill, *Utilitarianism: With Related Remarks from Mill's Other Writings*
(Hackett, 2017) and a co-editor of *Moral Theory and Climate Change: Ethical Perspectives on
a Warming Planet* (Routledge, 2020), *The Cambridge Companion to Utilitarianism*
(Cambridge, 2014), and *John Stuart Mill and the Art of Life* (Oxford, 2011). He is also the
author of numerous articles and book chapters on various topics in ethics.

Dale E. Miller

Old Dominion University, Virginia

Dale E. Miller is a professor of philosophy at Old Dominion University. He is the author of
John Stuart Mill: Moral, Social and Political Thought (Polity, 2010) and a co-editor of *Moral
Theory and Climate Change: Ethical Perspectives on a Warming Planet* (Routledge, 2020),
A Companion to Mill (Blackwell, 2017), *The Cambridge Companion to Utilitarianism*
(Cambridge, 2014), *John Stuart Mill and the Art of Life* (Oxford, 2011), and *Morality, Rules,
and Consequences: A Critical Reader* (Edinburgh, 2000). He is also the editor-in-chief of
Utilitas, and the author of numerous articles and book chapters on various topics in ethics
broadly construed.

About the Series

This Elements series provides an extensive overview of major figures, theories,
and concepts in the field of ethics. Each entry in the series acquaints students with the
main aspects of its topic while articulating the author's distinctive viewpoint in a manner
that will interest researchers.

Cambridge Elements ≡

Ethics

Elements in the Series

A full series listing is available at: www.cambridge.org/EETH

Lightning Source UK Ltd.
Milton Keynes UK
UKHW020240301122
413100UK00018B/261